Envision It! | Visual Skills Handbook

Author's Purpose

Cause and Effect

Classify and Categorize

Compare and Contrast

Details and Facts

Draw Conclusions

Fact and Opinion

Graphic Sources

Main Idea and Details

Sequence

Steps in a Process

Literary Elements

Author's Purpose

Authors write to inform or entertain.

To Inform

To Entertain

Cause and Effect

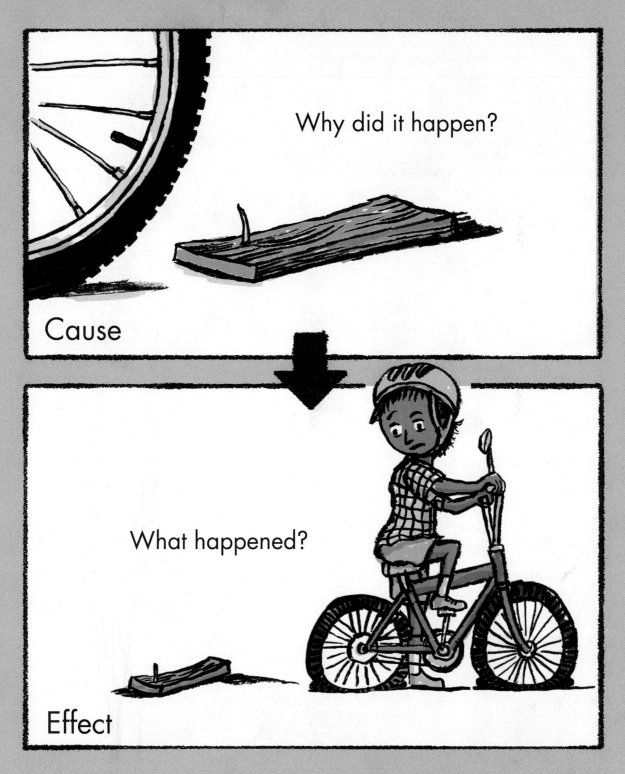

Why did it happen?

Cause

What happened?

Effect

Classify and Categorize

Which toys belong together?

Spaceships

Action figures

Compare and Contrast

How are
we alike?

How are
we different?

Details and Facts

Draw Conclusions

Use what you already know to help you understand what is happening.

Fact and Opinion

A statement of fact can be proven true or false.

That movie is about the Wright Brothers.

Fact

A statement of opinion tells someone's ideas or feelings.

Opinion

Graphic Sources

Time Line

How I Get Ready for School

6:30   7:00   7:30   8:00   8:30   9:00

Circle Graph

How We All Get There

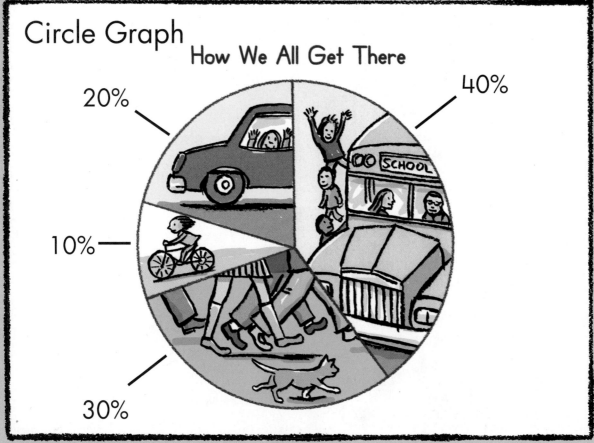

20%

40%

10%

30%

Main Idea and Details

Main Idea

What is the selection all about?

Details

Sequence

What happens first, next, and last?

Steps in a Process

1

2

3

4

Literary Elements

Characters

Plot

Beginning

Middle

End

What happens in the beginning, middle, and end of the story?

Problem/Solution

Problem

Solution

Setting

Where and when does the story take place?

Theme

What is the big idea in the story?

Envision It! | Visual Strategies Handbook

Background Knowledge

Background knowledge is what you already know about a topic. Use background knowledge before, during, and after reading to monitor your comprehension.

Let's Think About Reading!

When I use background knowledge, I ask myself
- What do I already know?
- What does this remind me of?
- What other stories does this make me think of?

Important Ideas

Important ideas are essential ideas and supporting details in a selection. Important ideas include information and facts that provide clues to the author's purpose.

Let's **Think** About **Reading!**

When I identify important ideas, I ask myself
- What are the important facts?
- What do the illustrations and photos show?
- What do diagrams and charts show that might be important?

Inferring

When we **infer** we use background knowledge with clues in the text to come up with our own ideas. We do this to support understanding.

Let's Think About Reading!

When I infer, I ask myself
- What do I already know?
- How does this help me understand what happened?

Monitor and Clarify

We **monitor** comprehension to make sure our reading makes sense. We **clarify** to find out why we haven't understood. Then we fix up problems.

This is hard to understand. I'll reread to figure it out.

Let's Think About Reading!

When I monitor and clarify, I ask myself
- Do I understand what I'm reading?
- What doesn't make sense?
- How can I fix it?

Predict and Set Purpose

We **predict** to tell what might happen next in a story or article. The prediction is based on what has already happened. We **set a purpose** to guide our reading.

Let's Think About Reading!

When I predict and set a purpose, I ask myself
- What do I already know?
- What do I think will probably happen next?
- What is my purpose for reading?

Questioning

Questioning is asking good questions about important text information. Questioning takes place before, during, and after reading.

How fast *does* it go?

Let's Think About Reading!

When I question, I ask myself
- What will this be about?
- What does the author mean?
- What questions help me make sense of what I'm reading?

Story Structure

Story structure is the arrangement of a story from beginning to end. We use the structure to retell important events in a story.

Let's Think About Reading!

When I identify story structure, I ask myself
- What happens in the beginning?
- What happens in the middle?
- What happens at the end?
- How can I use this to retell the story?

Summarize

When we **summarize,** we use our own words to retell the most important ideas or events of what we've read. A summary is no more than a few sentences.

Let's **Think** About **Reading!**

When I summarize, I ask myself
- What is this mostly about?
- What does the author mean?
- How is the information organized?

Text Structure

We use **text structure** with nonfiction to describe how information is organized, for example, by cause and effect or sequence. Notice text structure before, during, and after reading.

Let's Think About Reading!

When I identify text structure, I ask myself
- How is the text organized? Cause and effect? Sequence? Others?
- How does structure help me describe the order of the text?

Visualize

When we **visualize**, we form pictures in our minds about what happens in a story or article.

Let's Think About Reading!

When I visualize, I ask myself
- What do I already know?
- Which words and phrases create pictures in my mind?
- How does this help me understand what I'm reading?

SCOTT FORESMAN
READING STREET

GRADE 2

COMMON CORE

Program Authors

Peter Afflerbach

Camille Blachowicz

Candy Dawson Boyd

Elena Izquierdo

Connie Juel

Edward Kame'enui

Donald Leu

Jeanne R. Paratore

P. David Pearson

Sam Sebesta

Deborah Simmons

Susan Watts Taffe

Alfred Tatum

Sharon Vaughn

Karen Kring Wixson

Glenview, Illinois

Boston, Massachusetts

Chandler, Arizona

Hoboken, New Jersey

PEARSON

We dedicate Reading Street to
Peter Jovanovich.

His wisdom, courage,
and passion for education
are an inspiration to us all.

Accelerated Reader®

Acknowledgments appear on pages 548–549, which constitute an extension of this copyright page.

PEARSON

ISBN-13: 978-0-328-72450-5
ISBN-10:   0-328-72450-5
11 12 13 14 15 16 17 18 V057 18 17 16 15

Dear Reader,

Has your trip down *Scott Foresman Reading Street* been exciting so far? We hope so. Are you ready for more reading adventures? In this book, you will find out about pumpkins and soil and how a lost frog finds his way home. You will read about baseball, cowboys, our country's flag, and a boy who gets into trouble making signs.

Each time you turn a corner, you will learn something new. But you will also have many chances to use what you learned before. We hope you will have fun doing it.

Sit back and enjoy the trip!

Sincerely,
The Authors

Unit 4 Contents

Our Changing World

How do things change? How do they stay the same?

Week 1

Let's **Think** About **Reading!**

Unit 4 Contents

Week 6

Envision It! A Comprehension Handbook

Envision It! Visual Skills
Handbook EI•1–EI•15

Envision It! Visual Strategies
Handbook EI•17–EI•27

Words! Vocabulary Handbook W•1–W•15

Unit 5 Contents

Responsibility

What does it mean to be responsible?

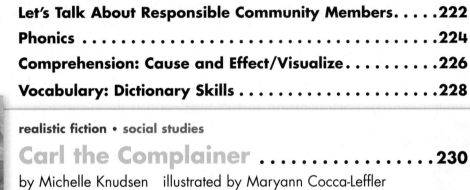

Week 2

Week 3

Unit 5 Contents

Week 6

Interactive Review
Reader's and Writer's Notebook . . .445–476

 **Envision It!** A Comprehension Handbook

 **Envision It! Visual Skills
Handbook EI•1–EI•15**

**Envision It! Visual Strategies
Handbook EI•17–EI•27**

Words! Vocabulary Handbook W•1–W•15

Unit 6 Contents

Are traditions and celebrations important in our lives?

Traditions

Week 1

Let's **Think** About **Reading!**

realistic fiction • social studies

by Angela Johnson   illustrated by Beth Peck

expository text • social studies

by Tammy Terry   illustrated by Clint Hansen

Week 2

Week 3

Unit 6 Contents

Week 6

Interactive Review

Reader's and Writer's Notebook . . . 541–572

Envision It! A Comprehension Handbook

Envision It! Visual Skills Handbook EI•1–EI•15

Envision It! Visual Strategies Handbook EI•17–EI•27

Words! Vocabulary Handbook W•1–W•15

READING STREET The Digital Path!

Don Leu
The Internet Guy

Right before our eyes, the nature of reading and learning is changing. The Internet and other technologies create new opportunities, new solutions, and new literacies. New reading comprehension skills are required online. They are increasingly important to our students and our society.

Those of us on the Reading Street team are here to help you on this new, and very exciting, journey.

See It!

- Big Question Video

- Concept Talk Video

- Envision It! Animations

- eReaders

- Interactive Sound-Spelling Cards

butterfly

b

Hear It!

- *Sing with Me Animations*

- eSelections

- Grammar Jammer

The dogs run and bark.
The duck flew.
The dog is running.
The dog is tired.

- Vocabulary Activities

16

Concept Talk Video

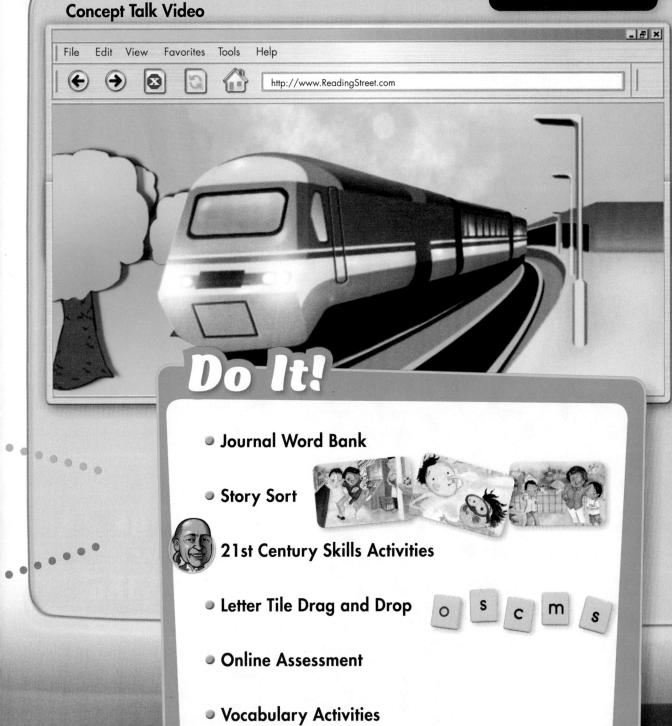

File   Edit   View   Favorites   Tools   Help

http://www.ReadingStreet.com

Do It!

- Journal Word Bank

- Story Sort

- 21st Century Skills Activities

- Letter Tile Drag and Drop

- Online Assessment

- Vocabulary Activities

Our Changing World

How do things change? How do they stay the same?

Common Core State Standards

Language 6. Use words and phrases acquired through conversations, reading and being read to, and responding to texts, including using adjectives and adverbs to describe (e.g., *When other kids are happy that makes me happy*). **Also Speaking/Listening 1.**

Oral Vocabulary

Let's Talk About

Help with Changes

- Share information about kinds of changes.

- Share ideas about the effects of changes and things that help us accept them.

READING STREET ONLINE
CONCEPT TALK VIDEO
www.ReadingStreet.com

You've learned
1 2 1
Amazing Words
so far this year!

21

Common Core State Standards
Foundational Skills 3. Know and apply grade-level phonics and word analysis skills in decoding words.

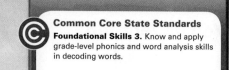

candle

syllable -le

Phonics

Final Syllable -*le*

Words I Can Blend

little

table

apple

bottle

bundle

Sentences I Can Read

1. Can we eat this little snack at my table?

2. He'll eat an apple and drink that bottle of water after his run.

3. Mom will bundle up newspapers and get them ready to recycle.

I Can Read!

"Listen to that odd whistle!" I didn't hear it. Jackson was trying to startle me, I could tell. He tries to scare his little brother at times. Jackson and I fiddle around a lot, but we made this simple pact. We're brothers and we're best pals.

We sat in the middle of a park when I felt something tumble from a maple tree, hit my head, and land in a puddle. "Let's get out!" Jackson yelled, more than a little scared.

As we ran, we saw a duck stumble by. That tumble scared him even more than us.

You've learned

○ Final Syllable -le

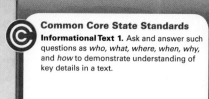

Common Core State Standards
Informational Text 1. Ask and answer such questions as *who, what, where, when, why,* and *how* to demonstrate understanding of key details in a text.

Skill

Draw Conclusions

Use what you already know to help you understand what is happening.

EI•7 9

Strategy

Envision It! Visual Strategies Handbook

Background Knowledge

Background knowledge is what you already know about a topic. Use background knowledge before, during, and after reading to monitor your comprehension.

When I use background knowledge, I ask myself
• What do I already know?
• What does this remind me of?
• What other stories does this make me think of?

EI•18

Comprehension Skill

Draw Conclusions

- When you read, you can draw conclusions or figure out more about the characters and events in a story.

- Use evidence, or proof, from the text to draw conclusions.

- Use what you learned about drawing conclusions and complete a graphic organizer like the one below as you read "Tadpoles to Frogs."

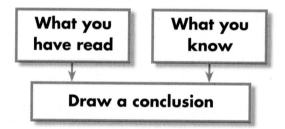

What you have read	What you know

↓   ↓

Draw a conclusion

Comprehension Strategy

Background Knowledge

Background knowledge is what you already know about a topic through your experiences or from other readings. Good readers use background knowledge to monitor, or check, understanding and then adjust that understanding.

Tadpoles to Frogs

What do you picture when you think of frogs? Maybe it's their long back legs. Maybe it's their loud croak. Maybe it's their lightning fast tongues that they use to catch bugs.

Strategy Think about what you already know about frogs.

You might be surprised to see what a frog looks like when it hatches. Then, it is a tadpole. Tadpoles are hatched in the water. They look almost like fish. Most tadpoles don't have legs. They swim by moving their tails.

The water is full of creatures that eat tadpoles. However, tadpoles can be very fast. This makes them hard to catch. Others sit very still and hide. This makes them hard to find. As tadpoles get older, they start to grow legs. They also grow lungs, organs that help them to breathe air. Finally the change is complete. A frog climbs out of the water. Ribbit!

Skill What changes have to happen for a frog to be able to live on land?

Your Turn!

Ⅱ Need a Review? See the *Envision It! Handbook* for additional help with draw conclusions and background knowledge.

Let's Think About..

▷ Ready to Try It? As you read *A Froggy Fable* on pp. 28–41, use what you've learned to understand the text.

Common Core State Standards

Language 4.a. Use sentence-level context as a clue to the meaning of a word or phrase.

perfect

pond

splashing

clearing
crashed
spilling
traveled

Vocabulary Strategy for

Multiple-Meaning Words

Context Clues You may come across a word you know, but the meaning doesn't fit in the sentence. The word may have more than one meaning. For example, *bank* means "a place to keep money." *Bank* also means "the ground along a river." You can use the context clues to figure out the word's relevant meaning.

1. Try the meaning you know. Does it make sense? If not, the word may have more than one meaning.

2. Read on and look at the nearby words. Can you figure out another meaning?

3. Try the new meaning in a sentence. Does it make sense?

Read "Life in a Pond." Use context clues to find the meanings of the multiple-meaning words.

Words to Write Reread "Life in a Pond." Write about your favorite place to go swimming. Use words from the *Words to Know* list.

Life in a Pond

It's up there, just beyond the forest. Can you hear it? Look past the trees into the open clearing. Do you see it? It's a pond, and it's full of all different kinds of plant and animal life. A pond is a small, quiet body of water. Don't let the size fool you though. Many different kinds of creatures live under the water or by the shore.

Look! Did you see that splashing? That was just a few fish going after an insect for lunch. And look over there, in the reeds by the shore! Do you see that turtle napping? Many of these animals were born here. Others came from far away. Look at that small stream spilling into the pond on the other side. Some of the animals traveled here by swimming in that stream.

Oh my gosh! What was that bang? Oh, it was the sound of that tree as it crashed into the water. Beavers did that. They are blocking off, or damming, parts of the pond. This makes it easier for them to get food.

For many animals, a pond is the perfect place to live.

Your Turn!

⏸ **Need a Review?** For more help with context clues and multiple-meaning words, see *Words!* on pp. W•7 and W•10.

Let's Think About..

▶ **Ready to Try It?** Read *A Froggy Fable* on pp. 28–41.

A Froggy Fable

by John Lechner

A **fable** is a story that teaches a lesson. Now read to find out what lesson the frog learns.

Question of the Week

How can familiar things help us with changes?

Once there was a frog who lived under a rock by himself.

Every day he did the same thing.

Let's **Think** About...

This story is about a frog. What do you know about frogs?

◉ Background Knowledge

He swam into the pond to eat breakfast.

30

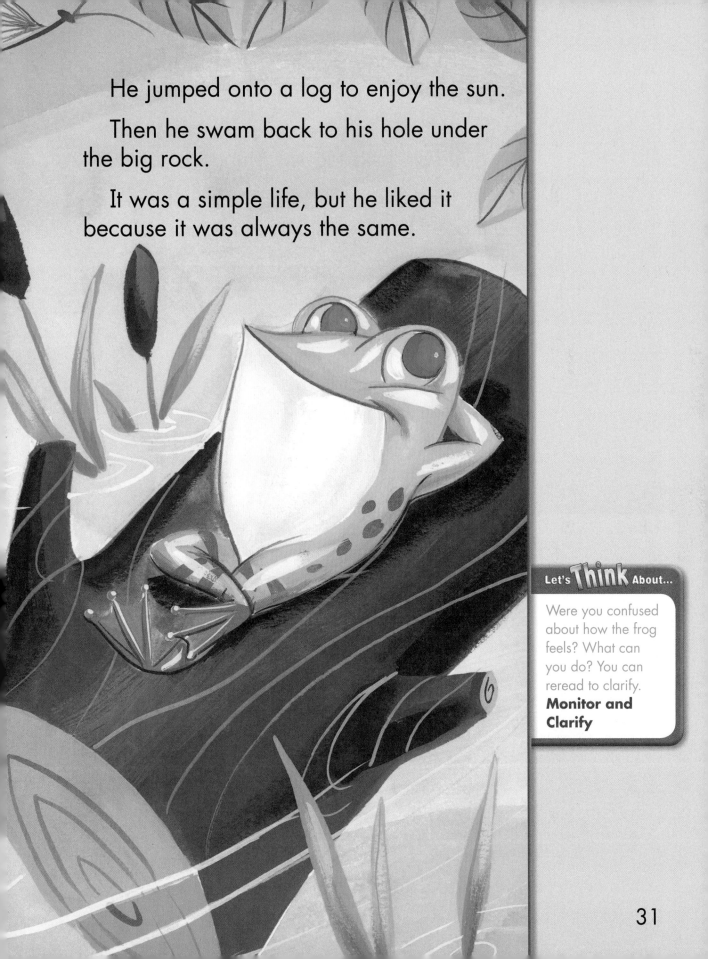

He jumped onto a log to enjoy the sun.

Then he swam back to his hole under the big rock.

It was a simple life, but he liked it because it was always the same.

Let's **Think** About...

Were you confused about how the frog feels? What can you do? You can reread to clarify. **Monitor and Clarify**

Then one day, things started to change. . . .

A family of otters moved into the pond and started splashing around.

"Hey," said the frog, "I don't like those otters splashing in my pond."

Let's Think About...

How do you feel when others get in your things? How does the frog feel about the otters? Do you feel the same way?

🄫 Background Knowledge

A flock of blue jays moved into the trees overhead, and they squawked ALL the time.

"Hey, I don't like those birds making noise," the frog said.

And one day, lightning struck
the tallest pine tree, which crashed
into the water, spilling pine needles
everywhere.

"Hey, I don't like that tree in my
pond!" said the frog.

But there was nothing he could do
about it.

The frog crawled into the back of
his hole and stayed there.

He heard a voice behind him.

"Why are you so sad?" It was a small caterpillar.

"I'm sad because everything is changing," said the frog.

"I'm glad things change," the caterpillar replied. "Someday I hope to change into a butterfly. Trees change . . . flowers change . . . even mountains and mighty rivers."

The frog just turned back toward the wall—he wanted to cry.

The caterpillar left, but the frog stayed in his hole.

Let's Think About...

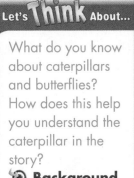

What do you know about caterpillars and butterflies? How does this help you understand the caterpillar in the story?
◉ Background Knowledge

34

Then one morning, something utterly unexpected happened. . . .

The rock over the frog's hole was lifted into the air.

To the poor frog's bewilderment, a jar came down on top of him . . . and he was whisked away in the hands of a young boy.

Needless to say, nothing like this had ever happened to the frog before.

The terrified frog was jostled and bumped on the boy's bike.

They traveled a long time, when suddenly the bike hit a rock. . . .

Let's **Think** About...

Are you confused about anything? What can you do to clarify? **Monitor and Clarify**

The jar went flying, and the frog fell behind some tall weeds. He sat very still until it was safe.

When the frog finally crept out, he found himself in a strange and unfamiliar place. He was lost.

Let's **Think** About...

How would you feel if you were away from home? How does the frog feel?

◉ **Background Knowledge**

37

The frog wandered until it got dark, then took shelter for the night in a hollow tree.

The next morning he kept on hopping, but just seemed to get more lost. Weeks went by, and the frog encountered many dangers . . . and many wonders.

Then one afternoon, when he had just about given up all hope of finding his home, he heard a noise from far away—a familiar noise.

He raced through the forest toward the sound.

Let's **Think** About...

The frog hears a familiar noise. What kind of noise would be familiar to him? What can you do to clarify? You can look back to find out.

Monitor and Clarify

39

As he got closer, he heard splashing.

Finally, he emerged into a clearing . . . and saw a beautiful pond. HIS pond.

Let's Think About...

Why is the frog happy to hear the sounds that once bothered him?
Inferring

He was so happy to see the blue jays flapping overhead.

He was so happy to see the otters splashing in the water.

He was even happy to see the fallen tree, right where he'd left it—he knew he was home.

True, his old rock had been torn away, but he found a perfect spot to dig another hole, with an even better view.

After that day, the frog didn't mind so much when things changed—he could handle anything.

He even tried something new once in a while.

And things were never the same again.

Let's Think About...

What happens in this story? Why does the frog change his ideas about change?
Summarize

Common Core State Standards

Literature 1. Ask and answer such questions as *who, what, where, when, why,* and *how* to demonstrate understanding of key details in a text. **Also Literature 2., Writing 1.**

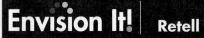

Envision It! Retell

Think Critically

1. Every day, the frog did the same thing. What are some things you do every day? **Text to Self**

2. How did the frog feel about changes at the end of the story? What lesson does the author teach with this story? **Think Like an Author**

3. How did the frog feel about the changes in his pond at the beginning of the fable? Why did the frog's feelings change after he returned home? **Draw Conclusions**

4. What do you know about frogs and where they live? Why would the frog need to live near a pond?

   Background Knowledge

5. **Look Back and Write** Look back at page 34. How does the caterpillar feel about changes? Use details from the selection as you write your answer.

   Key Ideas and Details • Text Evidence

Meet the Author

John Lechner

John Lechner is a writer, illustrator, and designer. Mr. Lechner grew up in Massachusetts with six brothers and sisters. At home, he took up music, while his brothers and sisters followed other creative interests. In college, Mr. Lechner studied creative writing and art.

A Froggy Fable is Mr. Lechner's first book. The story about a frog trying to handle changes in his life came from his own experiences. He has also written and illustrated a second children's story, *Sticky Burr: Adventures in Burrwood Forest*, about the adventures of a prickly burr and its friends. In addition to writing and illustrating children's stories, John Lechner designs games, Web sites, software, and animated films.

Read another book by John Lechner.

Sticky Burr: Adventures in Burrwood Forest

Use the *Reader's and Writer's Notebook* to record your independent reading.

43

Common Core State Standards
Writing 1. Write opinion pieces in which they introduce the topic or book they are writing about, state an opinion, supply reasons that support the opinion, use linking words (e.g., *because, and, also*) to connect opinion and reasons, and provide a concluding statement or section. **Also Language 1.e., 2.b.**

Let's Write It!

Key Features of a Friendly Letter

- has the date, greeting, body, closing, and signature
- the body of the letter expresses the message

READING STREET ONLINE
GRAMMAR JAMMER
www.ReadingStreet.com

Friendly Letter

A friendly letter can express ideas you want to write. Some friendly letters persuade the reader. The student model on the next page is an example of a friendly letter.

Writing Prompt Think about the new places the frog sees in his travels away from the pond. Write a friendly letter to the frog. Persuade him to visit a place that interests you.

Writer's Checklist

Remember, you should . . .

☑ begin your letter with a date and a greeting.

☑ give reasons to support your main idea.

☑ organize the reasons to persuade the reader.

☑ describe with adjectives.

February 9, 2010

Dear Frog,

Do you want to go to a fun place? Visit the Old Hills. The Old Hills have wide views.

A hill is a good place to hop or rest. It has hot days to keep you warm. The cool wind sounds like loud music. You can eat crunchy bugs. You will have a wonderful vacation.

Your friend,

Joe

Genre
This **friendly letter** has a date, greeting, body, closing, and signature.

Adjectives
can tell how something looks, sounds, or feels.

Writing Trait Organization
The writer gives one reason after another.

Conventions

Adjectives and Our Senses

Remember Adjectives describe people, places, and things. They can tell how things look, sound, taste, feel, or smell.

Aki wore a **soft tan** hat.

45

Genre
Tall Tale

- A tall tale is a story of unbelievable events told as if they were real.

- A tall tale is a story that uses exaggeration.

- A tall tale has characters doing impossible tasks.

- Read "Ben the Bullfrog." What events in the story show that the story is a tall tale?

Ben the Bullfrog
By Raquel Martinez

Ben the Bullfrog was the biggest frog around. At one, Ben was as big as a cat. By three, he was bigger than a cow. And he just kept growing! He outgrew his pond quickly.

He always dreamed of finding the perfect home. It had just the right amount of water. It had tall grass by the shore and big trees in the distance. Ben went out to find it.

Ben leaped from pond to pond, from river to river, and from lake to lake. All the ponds were just too little for him. No river was wide enough. No lake was deep enough. Ben didn't know where else to go.

A large heron flying overhead landed beside him. "What's wrong?" the heron asked.

"I'm looking for a home with grass and flowers and lots of water. But wherever I go, I'm always too big!"

The bird thought it over. "I heard of a place like the one you describe."

Let's Think About...

How is Ben the Bullfrog different from other bullfrogs?
Tall Tale

"Really?" Ben asked with excitement. "Where is it?"

"It's far north of here. You pass over the dry lands, through some forests, and through the prairie. You are going to the Great Lakes. From what I hear, you can't miss them."

"Great! I'll go now." Ben waited a minute before jumping.

"What's wrong?" the heron asked.

Ben looked around. "I've lived around here all my life. It's hard to leave."

Let's **Think** About...

What kind of details does the author use in the story? **Tall Tale**

The heron nodded. "Sometimes we outgrow our first homes. We have to move on. But we can always remember that place in our hearts." The bird reached over and picked a blue flower with its beak. "Here. Take this. It will remind you of what you left, and what you are looking for."

Ben smiled, took the flower, and hopped away.

Ben soon reached the dry land. The sand there was hot and hard to jump off. Ben began to leap across. Over time, his skin got dry and he became very thirsty. The dry land would be a very hard place to live, he thought.

Ben saw two lizards looking up at the sky. He stopped. "What are you looking at?" he asked.

"See those clouds up there?" one lizard said, pointing. "They fly over sometimes, but they never rain."

The second lizard nodded. "They say if you could tickle the clouds, then all the rain would fall out."

Ben looked up. "I could probably reach them."

"Really?"

Ben began to jump up and down. He jumped higher and higher. Soon he was high in the sky. He reached out and tickled a fluffy cloud. A couple of raindrops fell. The cloud laughed hard, and it began to rain. Then the cloud laughed harder, and there was a downpour.

The lizards were rolling and playing on the ground. "Thank you so much," they said. "Why don't you stay here and live with us?"

Ben had come far, but he still had not found a large lake. He remembered what the heron had said.

"No, thank you. I know where I have to go." Ben smiled and hopped away.

Let's Think About...

What could not really happen?
Tall Tale

49

The next day, Ben reached a forest. It had the tallest trees Ben had ever seen. He met a family of worried squirrels.

"What's wrong?" Ben asked.

"The trees are keeping all their nuts this year," the mama squirrel said. "They aren't letting any of them drop."

The papa squirrel nodded. "We need those nuts for the winter. "

Ben had an idea. "I might be able to help," he said.

Ben began to jump up and down. Each time he landed the Earth shook. It shook harder and harder until, finally, all the trees in the whole forest dropped their nuts.

The squirrels ran around with excitement.

"Thank you so much, Mr. Bullfrog," said the papa squirrel. "Why don't you stay here with us?"

Let's **Think** About...

What does Ben do to solve the problem that a real bullfrog could never do? **Tall Tale**

Ben thought about needing a bigger pond. He knew he had to keep searching.

"No, thank you. I know where I have to go." Ben smiled and hopped away.

Ben reached the prairie. It had grasses and flowers, but no trees. It was the longest stretch of open land he had ever seen. Finally, Ben jumped over a sandy hill and saw a huge lake. It was the biggest lake he had ever seen.

"This must be one of the Great Lakes!" he laughed.

Ben the Bullfrog took one great big leap down the hill. He planted his flower in the sandy hill. That way, he would always remember his home pond.

Then he jumped into the water. The lake wasn't too small, too shallow, or too narrow. It was perfect!
He was home.

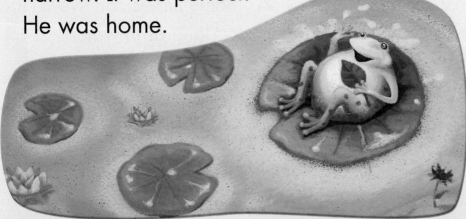

Let's **Think** About...

Reading Across Texts Think about the events in both *A Froggy Fable* and "Ben the Bullfrog." What events can really happen, and what events are make-believe?

Writing Across Texts Make a two-column chart. List all the true facts that the authors used in the stories on one side. On the other side, list all the ideas and events that are make-believe.

Common Core State Standards

Language 4.a. Use sentence-level context as a clue to the meaning of a word or phrase. **Also Foundational Skills 4.b.,** **Speaking/Listening 1., 1.a., 2.**

Let's Learn It!

Vocabulary

Multiple-Meaning Words

Context Clues Remember context clues can help you understand a multiple-meaning word's relevant meaning.

Practice It! Read and write each sentence. Determine the meaning for each bold word, and write it down.

1. The bus turned **right**.

2. The chef put the **top** on the pot.

Fluency

Read with Accuracy and Appropriate Rate

Read with accuracy. Be sure to read all the words. Do not omit or add words. Do not rush when you read. Read the sentences as if you are speaking.

Practice It!

1. Turtles are reptiles that have hard shells.

2. Some turtles can live on land or in water.

3. A tortoise is a turtle that lives only on land.

Media Literacy

Describe how media uses sound and graphics in messages.

Describe Media Techniques

Media uses graphics, words, sound, and motion to give messages. Sometimes the messages include facts and opinions. View media carefully. A message may be misleading. For example, a toothpaste ad may say that your smile will be bright when you use one brand of toothpaste. It may be, but your smile will probably be bright when you use any toothpaste. The ad is misleading.

Practice It! Work in groups. Find some ads on the Internet or in newspapers or magazines. Show the ads to the class. Use adjectives to describe the sounds and graphics used in them. Identify facts and opinions, and share whether any of the information is misleading. Speak clearly at an appropriate pace, using proper grammar. Follow classroom rules for discussion, including listening to others, speaking when it is your turn, and making appropriate contributions.

Common Core State Standards

Language 6. Use words and phrases acquired through conversations, reading and being read to, and responding to texts, including using adjectives and adverbs to describe (e.g., *When other kids are happy that makes me happy*).
Also Speaking/Listening 1.

Oral Vocabulary

Let's Talk About

Plants Changing

- Share information about the growth cycle of plants.

- Share ideas about what is needed for plants to change.

READING STREET ONLINE
CONCEPT TALK VIDEO
www.ReadingStreet.com

You've learned 1 2 9 Amazing Words so far this year!

55

© Common Core State Standards
Foundational Skills 3.b. Know spelling-
sound correspondences for additional
common vowel teams.

Envision It! | **Sounds to Know**

push

u

book

oo

READING STREET ONLINE
SOUND-SPELLING CARDS
www.ReadingStreet.com

Phonics

🎯 Vowel Patterns *oo, u*

Words I Can Blend

p u t

h o o k

l o o k

s t o o d

f u l l

Sentences I Can Read

1. Put my jacket on that hook.

2. Did she look at me when she stood on her head?

3. Eating that sandwich made me full.

I Can Read!

Cooking can be fun. It's best to learn from an adult. I took lessons from my mom. I'd look on when she followed recipes from her cookbook. It took a full month before I was ready to cook my first dish. The first dish I made was a grilled cheese sandwich. Mom stood next to me as I put cheese and butter on the bread. She helped me put it on the griddle and turn it when it was ready. That sandwich tasted so good!

You've learned

🔵 Vowel Patterns *oo, u*

Common Core State Standards

Informational Text 2. Identify the main topic of a multiparagraph text as well as the focus of specific paragraphs within the text. **Also Informational Text 3.**

Envision It! Skill Strategy

Skill

Envision It! Visual Skills Handbook

Sequence

What happens first, next, and last?

EI•12

Strategy

Important Ideas

Important ideas are essential ideas and supporting details in a selection. Important ideas include information and facts that provide clues to the author's purpose.

This is important information!

FIRE SAFETY
YOU ARE HERE

Let's Think About Reading!

When I identify important ideas, I ask myself
• What are the important facts?
• What do the illustrations and photos show?
• What do diagrams and charts show that might be important?

EI•19

READING STREET ONLINE
ENVISION IT! ANIMATIONS
www.ReadingStreet.com

Comprehension Skill

Sequence

• Sequence is the order that things happen in a story or article.

• Clue words such as *first* and *then* can help you learn the sequence of events.

• Use what you learned about sequence and use the graphic organizer to describe the order of events in "Life Cycle of an Oak."

First	Next	Last

Comprehension Strategy

Important Ideas

It is hard to remember all the details from one story. That is why good readers always look for important ideas. They are what you want to remember about a story. Important ideas can be found in the text of a story. Sometimes they can be found in bold words or in captions. Even titles can show important ideas. Locating facts and details in the text helps identify and support the ideas.

Life Cycle of an Oak

Even the biggest oak tree starts as a little acorn. Inside the acorn is a seed. To grow, the seed needs soil, water, and the right temperature.

Soon, the seed shell is broken. Roots grow down into the soil looking for food and water. A sprout grows out of the ground and looks for sunlight. The sprout grows and becomes a seedling. The seedling needs lots of food, water, and sunlight. The weather, animals, and disease can harm the young seedling.

Strategy What is the most important idea from this paragraph? Locate facts and details that helped you.

If the tree lives, it grows some more. Then, the young tree becomes a sapling. When people buy trees to plant, they buy saplings. Now the tree grows fast. It gets more branches. The roots spread out. Soon the tree is big. A mature tree can grow its whole life. Some oaks grow to be over 25 feet and live for over 200 years!

Skill Notice the clue word *then*. What does the word tell you about the tree's life cycle?

Your Turn!

Need a Review? See the *Envision It! Handbook* for additional help with sequence and important ideas.

Ready to Try It? As you read *Life Cycle of a Pumpkin*, use what you've learned to understand the text.

Common Core State Standards

Language 4.a. Use sentence-level context as a clue to the meaning of a word or phrase. **Also Language 5.**

⦿ Antonyms

Context Clues Antonyms are words that have opposite meanings. For example, *stop* is the opposite of *go*. When you do not know the meaning of a word, try looking at the context clues. The author may have used an antonym. It can help you figure out the meaning of the unfamiliar word.

1. If you do not know the meaning of a word in the sentence, look at the nearby words. The word may have an antonym.

2. The words "no" or "not" may signal an antonym for a word.

3. Use the antonym to help understand the meaning of the opposite word.

As you read "Great Grapes," identify antonyms. Use these words to figure out the meaning of each term.

Words to Write Reread "Great Grapes." What is your favorite fruit? Describe it. Use words from the *Words to Know* list.

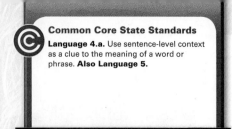

Great Grapes

Grapes are a kind of fruit. They are small and round. They grow on a vine. Grapes come in many different colors, such as green, red, white, black, and blue.

Grape farmers usually start with old vines, not new ones. They cut and save parts of the old vines. Then they plant the parts in the soil. The vine makes a root that pushes into the soil. The farmers hang wires between poles. The vines cling to the poles and grow up and across the wires. Vines use long, thin shoots to hold on as they climb. Some fruits grow very quickly. Grapevines work much more slowly. The vines do not grow grapes for several years. But once they start growing grapes, they can grow them every year for as long as one hundred years!

Grape harvest happens in the summer or fall. Farmers cut the grapes from the vines. Grapes for eating are put in boxes and shipped to market. Some are spread out on paper and left in the sun to dry. Soon they are no longer smooth. They have become small, bumpy raisins.

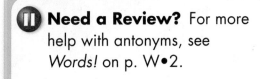

Your Turn!

⏸ **Need a Review?** For more help with antonyms, see *Words!* on p. W•2.

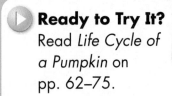

▷ **Ready to Try It?** Read *Life Cycle of a Pumpkin* on pp. 62–75.

Life Cycle of a Pumpkin

by Ron Fridell and Patricia Walsh

Genre

Expository text tells facts about a topic. Look for facts about how a pumpkin grows.

Question of the Week
How do plants change over time?

What is a pumpkin?

    A pumpkin is a fruit. It grows
on a vine like other kinds of squash. Pumpkins can
be bumpy or smooth, large or small, long or round.
They can be orange, white, yellow, or red.

    Each year there is a new crop of pumpkins.
Their hard shells have deep lines that go from
top to bottom.

Seed   1 week   2 weeks   10 weeks

Seed

Spring

Pumpkins begin as seeds. The seeds are white and have an oval shape. A tiny plant is curled up inside each seed.

The seed is planted in warm, moist soil. In about ten days, a root grows down into the soil. The root takes in water and food for the plant. Tiny leaves push up into the sunlight.

11 weeks

14 weeks

16 weeks

Seedling

The first two leaves pop through the soil. These are smooth seed leaves. They use sunlight and air to make food for the new plant.

Then the true leaves appear. They are jagged and prickly. The job of the seed leaves is done. They wither and fall off.

Seed   1 week   2 weeks   10 weeks

Vine

The pumpkin plant grows more leaves. The plant grows quickly and soon becomes a vine. The vine twists and creeps along the ground.

The vine sends out thin tendrils. They grab and curl around other vines. They twist around fences. The tendrils support the vine as it grows longer and longer.

11 weeks

14 weeks

16 weeks

Flower

The pumpkin vine blooms with many yellow flowers. Some of these are female flowers. Female flowers sit on small, fuzzy, green balls.

Other flowers are male flowers. They are on long stems and have yellow powder inside the flower. The yellow powder is pollen. It takes a male and a female flower to make a pumpkin.

Seed

1 week

2 weeks

10 weeks

Pollination

It also takes bees to make pumpkins. They move the pollen from male flowers to female flowers. When a bee visits the male flowers, the pollen sticks to the bee's body and legs.

The pollen rubs off the bee as it goes in and out of the flowers. When the pollen reaches a female flower, the fuzzy green ball at the end of the flower begins to grow into a pumpkin.

11 weeks

14 weeks

16 weeks

Growing and ripening

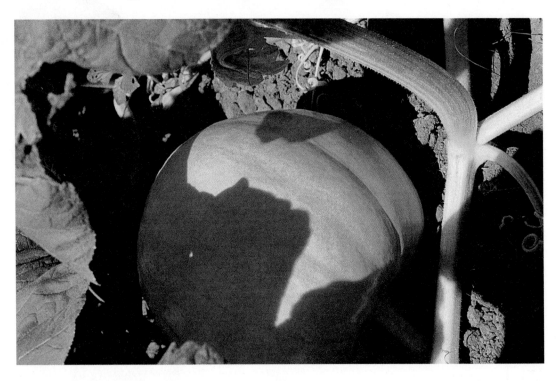

All summer the vines, tendrils, and leaves of the plant grow and tangle together. Underneath the big leaves are little pumpkins.

The leaves are like big umbrellas. They keep the hot sun off the pumpkins. They also help to keep the soil around the pumpkins from drying out.

Seed

1 week

2 weeks

10 weeks

Problems for pumpkins

Growing pumpkins need just the right amount of water and sun. Too much rain rots the pumpkins. Too much sun withers the vines.

Cucumber beetles and squash bugs can hurt pumpkins too. Farmers spray the plant with insecticides or cover the vines with nets to protect the growing pumpkins.

11 weeks

14 weeks

16 weeks

The pumpkins grow bigger
and bigger. Inside, the pumpkins
form seeds and pulp. Outside,
the pumpkins turn from green
to orange.

Then the vines turn brown. Harvest
time has come. The farmer cuts the thick
pumpkin stem from the vine.

Seed

1 week

2 weeks

10 weeks

After the harvest

Four months ago there were only seeds. Now the farmer has harvested a wagon full of round, orange pumpkins. They will be sold at farmstands and stores.

People cook pumpkins and use the pulp to make pumpkin pie, cookies, soup, and bread. Some pumpkins are fed to farm animals.

11 weeks

14 weeks

16 weeks

73

Festivals

 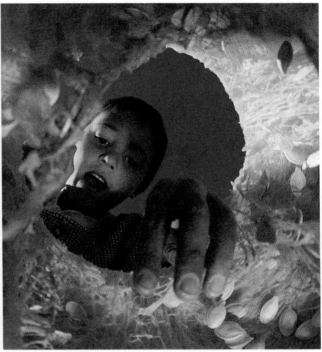

Some towns hold a pumpkin festival to celebrate the fall harvest. Sometimes there is a contest to find out who grew the biggest pumpkin.

Inside the pumpkin are many seeds. Some seeds are roasted to be eaten as a snack. Other seeds are saved to be planted in the spring. They will grow into next year's pumpkins.

Seed

1 week

2 weeks

10 weeks

Next year's crop

After the pumpkins are picked and sold, the farmer plows the field. Old vines and unpicked pumpkins get mixed with the soil. The field is ready for planting seeds again next spring.

11 weeks

14 weeks

16 weeks

Common Core State Standards

Informational Text 1. Ask and answer such questions as *who, what, where, when, why,* and *how* to demonstrate understanding of key details in a text.
Also Informational Text 2., 6., Writing 2.

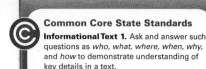

Envision It! Retell

Think Critically

1. How have you and your family used a pumpkin? Text to Self

2. What do you think the authors want readers to learn about pumpkins? Think Like an Author

3. What does a pumpkin plant get first, roots or flowers? Sequence

4. Look at the first paragraph on page 71. Which sentence gives the paragraph's most important idea? Important Ideas

5. Look Back and Write Look back at page 69. How do bees help pumpkin plants? Provide evidence to support your answer.

Key Ideas and Details • Text Evidence

Meet the Author

Ron Fridell and Patricia Walsh

Ron Fridell and Patricia Walsh are married, and they are both writers. They often write their own books, but they wrote *Life Cycle of a Pumpkin* together.

Mr. Fridell and Ms. Walsh do lots of research. They use the library and the Internet, but they like to see things themselves too. When they were doing research for this book, they went to a pumpkin festival in Illinois.

Mr. Fridell and Ms. Walsh love to travel. "We travel for adventure and the excitement of seeing new places. But we also travel to do research and get ideas for our books."

Read two more books by Ron Fridell and Patricia Walsh.

Life Cycle of a Spider

Life Cycle of a
Spider

Life Cycle of a
Turtle

Life Cycle of a Turtle

Reading Log

Use the *Reader's and Writer's Notebook* to record your independent reading.

Common Core State Standards

Writing 2. Write informative/explanatory texts in which they introduce a topic, use facts and definitions to develop points, and provide a concluding statement or section. **Also Language 1.e.**

Let's Write It!

Key Features of Expository Nonfiction

- explains an object or an idea
- uses facts and details
- sometimes uses graphic features such as maps or diagrams

Expository Nonfiction

Expository nonfiction tells facts about a topic. The student model on the next page is an example of expository nonfiction.

Writing Prompt Think about something in nature that changes during a year. Now write an explanation of how it changes from season to season.

Writer's Checklist

Remember, you should . . .

☑ give facts and details.

☑ choose words that make your writing clear.

☑ use descriptive adjectives and articles correctly.

The Oak Tree

A tall oak tree grows from one small round acorn. The tree stands, full of leaves, reaching up to the sky.

In the fall, the leaves change. They turn many colors and then fall.

The big tree stays in the winter without leaves. In spring, green leaves grow back.

Adjectives can tell how many, what size, and what shape.

Writing Trait Word Choice The writer uses words that make the ideas clear.

Genre Expository nonfiction gives facts and details.

Conventions

- ## Adjectives for Number, Size, and Shape
- **Remember Adjectives** (such as *two, huge,* and *round*) can tell the number, size, and shape of things. The words **a, an,** and **the** are adjectives called **articles**.

Common Core State Standards
Literature 4. Describe how words and phrases (e.g., regular beats, alliteration, rhymes, repeated lines) supply rhythm and meaning in a story, poem, or song.

Science in Reading

Genre
Poetry

- Poetry has words written in lines with rhythm, or a beat.

- Rhyming poems have lines that end with the same sounds.

- Poems often repeat their rhythm or rhymes.

- Poetry helps you think about what you see, hear, feel, and know.

- Read "How do seeds know which way is up?" Look and listen for the rhythm, rhymes, and repetition that make it poetry.

- Look back at another poem by Amy Goldman Koss (Volume 1, page 448). How are the settings of the two poems alike and different?

80

How do seeds know which way is UP?

by Amy Goldman Koss

It's dark underground
Where sunlight can't go,
So how does a seed
Know which way to grow?

The root is the first
To grow from the seed—
Down into the darkness
It digs at full speed.

Gravity sensors
Within each young root
Teach it to follow
A straight downward route.

And once this young root
Has taken the lead,
A tender green shoot
Sprouts out of the seed.

The shoot only knows
That its life's pursuit
Means heading the opposite
Way of the root.

Since shoots need the sunlight
To live and to grow,
They force themselves upward
Through dark dirt below.

The roots need the water
And the shoots need the light.
Each goes its own way,
And that works out just right!

Let's Think About...

What words **rhyme** in the poem? How does that affect the **rhythm** of the poem? Can you picture seeds growing?

Let's Think About...

Reading Across Texts How is the plant in this poem like the pumpkin plant you read about in *Life Cycle of a Pumpkin*?

Writing Across Texts Draw a diagram of a seed sprouting into a plant. Label your diagram.

81

Common Core State Standards

Speaking/Listening 4. Tell a story or recount an experience with appropriate facts and relevant, descriptive details, speaking audibly in coherent sentences. **Also Foundational Skills 4.b., Speaking/Listening 1., Language 1.e., 4.a., 5.**

Let's
Learn
It!

READING STREET ONLINE
ONLINE STUDENT EDITION
www.ReadingStreet.com

Get Ready For Grade 3

Listen carefully to announcements.

Listening and Speaking

Make an Announcement

You make announcements to share important information. Speak clearly when making announcements. Speak loud enough and at an appropriate pace so everyone can hear you. Listen closely to others.

Practice It! Make an announcement. Tell the class what time school starts. Share with the class what you will do before school starts. Take turns. Listen carefully to the other announcements.

Tips

• Use future tense verbs in your announcement.

• Use descriptive adjectives like *wonderful*, articles like *a*, *an*, and *the*, and adverbs about time, like *before* and *next*, in your announcement.

82

Vocabulary

Antonyms

Context Clues If you don't know a word when you are reading, look for context clues. There might be an antonym that can help you figure out the meaning of the word.

Practice It! Read the paired sentences. Identify the antonyms using context clues. Then write your own sentences using the antonyms.

1. The car ride to school was bumpy. The road was not smooth.

2. My brother caught a huge fish. I only caught a tiny one.

Fluency

Read with Accuracy

When you read, say the word you see. Blend the sounds to read the word. Put the word in the sentence. Ask yourself if it makes sense.

Practice It! Read the sentences out loud.

1. Kara could not decide between the apples or the grapes.

2. That plant has long, green stems and red roses.

3. To grow, green plants need sun and water.

Common Core State Standards
Language 6. Use words and phrases acquired through conversations, reading and being read to, and responding to texts, including using adjectives and adverbs to describe (e.g., *When other kids are happy that makes me happy*).
Also Speaking/Listening 1.

Oral Vocabulary

Let's Talk About

Changes Under the Ground

- Share information about different kinds of soil.

- Share ideas about how plants, animals, people, and soil affect each other.

READING STREET ONLINE
CONCEPT TALK VIDEO
www.ReadingStreet.com

85

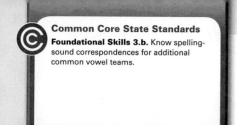

Common Core State Standards
Foundational Skills 3.b. Know spelling-
sound correspondences for additional
common vowel teams.

Envision It! | **Sounds to Know**

owl

ow

mouse

ou

oil

oi

boy

oy

READING STREET ONLINE
SOUND-SPELLING CARDS
www.ReadingStreet.com

Phonics

🎯 Diphthongs *ou, ow, oi, oy*

Words I Can Blend

couch

crowd

toy

noisemaker

playground

Sentences I Can Read

1. It's fun when my whole family can crowd onto this couch.

2. We gave him that toy as his gift.

3. She left her noisemaker on the playground.

Joy said to her friend Troy, "Wow! There is not a cloud in the sky! How about we go out and enjoy this beautiful day?"

Troy was a boy who was kind of a grouch. "Joy, did that loud noise last night spoil your sleep? It annoyed me. I just want to sit on the couch."

"Troy, you will enjoy being out," Joy said. "We can go to the playground."

"That might be a good choice," Troy decided.

"Troy, I'm proud of you!" Joy cheered.

You've learned

- Diphthongs *ou, ow, oi, oy*

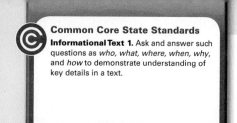

Common Core State Standards
Informational Text 1. Ask and answer such questions as *who, what, where, when, why,* and *how* to demonstrate understanding of key details in a text.

Envision It! | Skill Strategy

Skill

Strategy

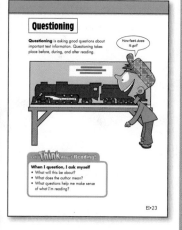

READING STREET ONLINE
ENVISION IT! ANIMATIONS
www.ReadingStreet.com

Comprehension Skill

Fact and Opinion

- A statement of fact can be proven true or false by checking a book or asking someone who knows.

- An opinion tells someone's feelings or ideas. Clue words such as *best* and *should* often show opinions.

- Use what you learned about locating facts and opinions and use a graphic organizer like this as you read "Good to Grow."

Fact	Opinion

Comprehension Strategy

Questioning

Good readers ask themselves questions as they read. Asking literal and relevant, or important, questions about the text can help you understand what you read. As you read, ask yourself if a sentence is a fact or an opinion. Ask, "Can this be proven true or false by checking it out?"

Good to **Grow**

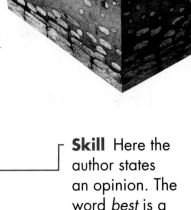

Have you ever wondered where dirt comes from? Dirt, or soil, starts out as rock. Over many, many years, the rock breaks down into smaller pieces. These pieces become part of the soil. If you could dig until you hit bedrock, you would dig through all the layers shown in the diagram. The diagram is the best way to show soil layers.

Skill Here the author states an opinion. The word *best* is a clue word.

In places such as Central Valley, California, the bedrock layer was made long ago by a volcano. Volcanic soil contains many nutrients. Nutrients are things plants need to live and grow. In a place with volcanic soil, you will probably see many farms. In fact, Central Valley farms grow much of our country's food.

Strategy Here is a good place to ask a question: Why are Central Valley farms a good place to grow food?

Your Turn!

Need a Review? See the *Envision It! Handbook* for additional help with fact and opinion and questioning.

Ready to Try It? As you read *Soil*, use what you've learned to understand the text.

Soil

Common Core State Standards
Language 4.c. Use a known root word as a clue to the meaning of an unknown word with the same root (e.g., *addition, additional*). **Also Foundational Skills 3.d.**

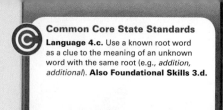

Envision It! | Words to Know

grains

substances

texture

materials
particles
seeps

Vocabulary Strategy for

◎ Suffixes

Word Structure When you read, you may come to a word you don't know. You might look for a suffix. Does the word have the suffix *-ful* at the end? The suffix *-ful* added to a word usually makes the word mean "full of ___." For example, *colorful* means "full of color." You may be able to use the suffix to help you figure out the meaning of the word.

1. Put your finger over the suffix *-ful*.

2. Look at the base word. Put the base word in the phrase "full of ___."

3. Try that meaning in the sentence. Does it make sense?

Read "Working with Soil." Look for words that end with *-ful*. Use the suffix to help you figure out the meanings of the words.

Words to Write Reread "Working with Soil." Did you learn anything new about soil? Write what you learned about soil. Use words from the *Words to Know* list.

Working with Soil

I love to make mud pies. First, I take some soil and put it in a pail. Then I add water. The water seeps through the soil and makes mud. The texture of the mud has to feel just right. I use my thumbs to make a jagged pie crust edge for the mud pie. Sometimes I put grains of sand over the top of the pie. The sand looks like sugar. Sometimes I put colorful flower petals on the pie to make it look nice. When I show my mother my mud pie, she pretends to eat it. I pour out the old mud until only a few particles of dirt are left in the pail. Then I start over again.

Even though I am older, I still make mud pies today! Now it is my job to work with materials like sand and dirt. I find helpful ways to make the soil better for growing plants. I try adding different substances to soil. Sometimes I add things, such as grass or leaves. Then I see how long it takes these things to decay. Farmers depend on people like me. I find the best ways to prepare soil for planting seeds.

Your Turn!

⏸ **Need a Review?** For more help with using suffixes to determine the meaning of a word, see *Words!* on p. W·6.

▷ **Ready to Try It?** Read *Soil* on pp. 92–109.

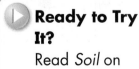

Soil

by Sally M. Walker

Question of the Week
What changes occur under the ground?

93

What Is Soil?

Did you ever make mud pies when you were little? If you did, soil was one of the ingredients you used. You may have called it dirt instead of soil.

Soil is in lots of places. You can find soil under the grass. It surrounds tree and flower roots. It lies beneath sidewalks and streets. If you could lift your house, you would probably find soil under it too!

A scoop of soil contains many things. Soil has rocks in it. Plants and bits of leaves are in soil. Many creatures live in soil too.

Soil is a natural resource. Natural resources are materials found on Earth that help living things. They are made by nature, not people. Soil helps plants and animals grow. They cannot live without it. But where does soil come from?

How Soil Forms

Soil is made up of different kinds of materials. One of these materials is bits of rock. Rocks are broken pieces of bedrock. Bedrock is the layer of solid rock that covers the outside of Earth.

Rocks are hard. But they can be broken into tiny bits. Tiny bits are called particles. Water, ice, and wind are strong enough to break rocks.

Rocks Become Soil

Hard rocks can break into small pieces.

Ice split this huge rock in half!

As water rushes down this hill, it breaks off bits of rock.

Rushing water in rivers makes rocks roll and tumble. The rocks break into smaller pieces. Tiny particles of rock break loose.

Rainwater seeps into cracks in rocks. If it gets cold enough, the water freezes. It becomes ice. Ice takes up more space than water. So the ice pushes against the rock. It makes the cracks bigger. Pieces of rock break off.

This glacier is flowing downhill. As it moves, it carries rocks with it.

Glaciers are giant, moving slabs of ice. Glaciers are very heavy. Their weight slowly grinds big rocks into small pieces.

Wind blows sand grains against big rocks. The sand grains scrub off particles of rock.

Rocks are made of minerals. A mineral is a hard substance made in nature. Minerals are not alive, like plants or animals. The minerals in a rock become part of the soil when the rock breaks apart.

Minerals are an important part of soil. They add nutrients to soil. Nutrients are substances that help living things grow. Soil contains nutrients that plants and animals need to stay healthy.

Copper nugget

There are many kinds of bacteria. They live nearly everywhere on Earth. This picture shows one kind of bacteria that lives in soil.

Humus is the second material that is in soil. Humus is dark brown or black. It is made of bits of dead plants and animals.

Humus is made by bacteria. Bacteria are tiny living things. They are so tiny that they can be seen only with a microscope. Microscopes are tools that make small things look big.

Bacteria eat dead plants and animals. They break the plants and animals into tiny pieces. The pieces become humus. Humus contains nutrients that had been inside the plants and animals. The nutrients can become part of the soil.

Air is the third material in soil. Soil is full of air spaces. Some air spaces are large. You can easily see them. You can see the tunnels that earthworms dig in soil. An earthworm's hole is filled with air. Soil also has tiny air spaces. The tiny spaces are between bits of minerals and humus. Most of these spaces are too small for you to see. But they are there.

Water is the fourth material found in soil. Water can move around in soil. It trickles through the soil's air spaces. The moving water picks up nutrients from the soil. The water carries the nutrients into roots of plants.

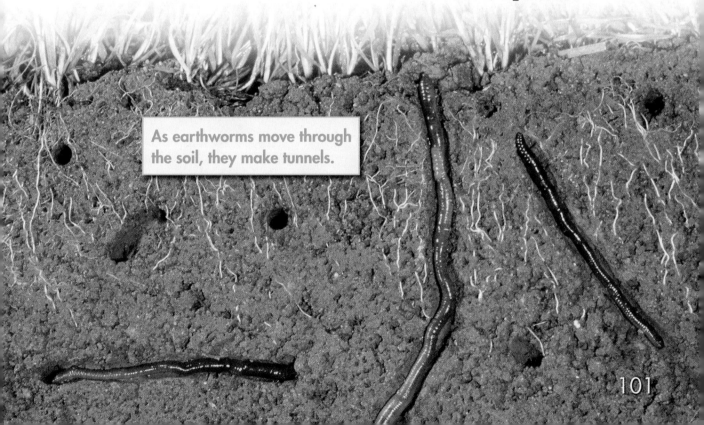

As earthworms move through the soil, they make tunnels.

Soil forms on flat land. It forms alongside rivers. It forms on forest floors and on low hills. Soil forms as humus and rock particles begin to pile up. It can take hundreds of years for 1 inch of soil to form.

Soil cannot form in some places. Soil cannot form on steep mountains. That's because soil-making materials slide down the mountain. Soil cannot form in very windy places or places where water flows quickly. In these places, soil-making materials can't pile up. They do not have enough time to become soil.

What Soil Looks Like

Soil can be made of many different kinds of minerals. Different minerals can be different colors. The minerals and humus in soil help give the soil its color. Many soils are a shade of brown. But some are yellow. Some are even bright orange-red.

Soil also has different textures. Texture is how rough or smooth something is. The texture of soil depends on the size of the soil's particles.

This picture shows sandy soil (left), loam (middle), and clay soil (right).

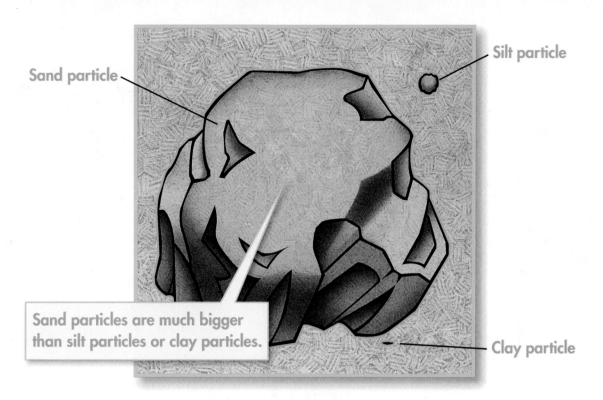

Sand particle

Silt particle

Sand particles are much bigger than silt particles or clay particles.

Clay particle

The largest mineral particles in soil are called sand. You can see the mineral particles in sandy soil. Sand particles feel rough when you rub them between your fingers. Some sand-sized particles have sharp, jagged edges. Others are mostly round.

Another kind of particle in soil is called silt. Silt particles are much smaller than sand particles. It's hard to see silt particles. If you rub silt between your fingers, it feels smooth. Silt-sized particles are shaped like sand particles.

Clay particles are the smallest particles in soil. They are too small to see without a microscope. Clay particles are flat.

Water drains quickly through sand. That's why you won't see puddles in wet sand at the beach.

Sand particles have big air spaces between them. Water drains quickly through the spaces. So puddles rarely form in sandy soil. Silt particles have smaller spaces between them. Water takes longer to drain through small spaces. Flat clay particles get squeezed together. The spaces between clay particles are tiny. Water has a hard time trickling through tiny air spaces. Clay particles also soak up water. So it takes a long time for water to drain through soil that has a lot of clay.

Water drains slowly through clay particles. When it rains, puddles often form in the soil that has many clay particles.

Soil with equal amounts of sand, silt, and clay particles is called loam. Loam is very good for growing plants. It holds just the right amount of water for growing roots.

Soil that has mostly sand-sized particles is called sandy loam. Water drains quickly through sandy loam.

Soil with mostly clay-sized particles is called clay loam. Water drains slowly through clay loam. Rain often forms puddles in clay loam.

What kind of texture does your soil have? Rub the soil between your fingers. Does it feel rough, smooth, or in-between?

Put some soil in your palm. Add a small amount of water to your soil. Add only enough to make the soil moist. If it seems too wet, add a little more soil. Mix the soil and water together with your fingers. See if you can mold the soil into a flat circle. If you can, your soil has a lot of clay. If the circle crumbles, the soil contains more sand and silt than clay.

The next time you go outside, look at the soil around you. Notice its color. See what kinds of plants are growing in it. Feel its texture.

Watch how people take care of the soil. Try to think of ways that you can care for the soil around your house. Plants, animals, and people will always need healthy soil!

Soybean field

109

Common Core State Standards
Informational Text 1. Ask and answer such questions as *who, what, where, when, why,* and *how* to demonstrate understanding of key details in a text.
Also Informational Text 3., Writing 2.

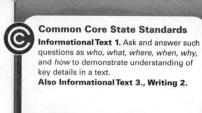

Think Critically

1. How was soil used in *Life Cycle of a Pumpkin*? Text to Text

2. Does the author think soil is important? How do you know?

Think Like an Author

3. Find a sentence in the article that gives a fact. How do you know it is a fact? Fact and Opinion

4. What questions did you ask yourself as you read about soil? What did you learn? Questioning

5. **Look Back and Write** Look back at page 95. What is in soil? Provide evidence to support your answer.

Key Ideas and Details • Text Evidence

Sally M. Walker

Sally M. Walker has won several awards for her writing. Most of her books are nonfiction. She especially enjoys writing about science. She says, "I enjoy finding odd snippets of information that get children 'turned on' to science."

Ms. Walker lives in Illinois with her husband, two children, a golden retriever, and two cats.

Read two more books by Sally M. Walker.

Bessie Coleman Daring to Fly

The 18 Penny Goose

Use the *Reader's and Writer's Notebook* to record your independent reading.

Reading Log

Common Core State Standards

Writing 2. Write informative/explanatory texts in which they introduce a topic, use facts and definitions to develop points, and provide a concluding statement or section. **Also Language 1.e., 6.**

Let's Write It!

Key Features of an Expository Report

- tells what you have learned about a topic
- includes facts and ideas about that topic
- sometimes uses graphic features such as pictures

READING STREET ONLINE
GRAMMAR JAMMER
www.ReadingStreet.com

Expository

Short Expository Report

A short **expository report** tells facts and details that the writer has learned about a topic. The student model on the next page is an example of a short expository report.

Writing Prompt Think about what you have learned about soil. Now write a short report describing the soil in your neighborhood.

Writer's Checklist

Remember, you should . . .

☑ tell facts and details you learn about the topic.

☑ use short and long sentences that make your report clear.

☑ use adjectives to describe soil.

112

Soil in My Neighborhood

The soil by my house is dry, and water sinks right in. There is a lot of sand in the soil. In some places the dirt is sandier than in other places.

The dirt in my yard is darker than dirt in the park. The park soil looks older. The community garden has the darkest soil of all.

Writing Trait Sentences
Writer uses the word *and* to tell two related facts in one sentence.

Genre
This short **expository report** tells facts about soil.

Adjectives
with *-er* and *-est* compare kinds of soil.

Conventions

Adjectives That Compare

- **Remember** Add **-er** to an adjective to compare two things. Add **-est** to an adjective to compare three or more things.

- This is the **smallest** bit of all the rocks. Sand is **smaller** than gravel.

113

Common Core State Standards
Informational Text 2. Identify the main topic of a multiparagraph text as well as the focus of specific paragraphs within the text. **Also Informational Text 5., 6.**

Science in Reading

Genre
Expository Text

- Expository text tells facts about a topic.

- The topic may be about real people, animals, places, or things.

- Expository text often has text features like headings to locate information.

- Captions next to photographs also help to locate specific information.

- Read "Burrowing Animals." Notice how the headings help you to know what is coming next in the text.

Burrowing Animals
by Penny Dowdy

Gophers and Prairie Dogs

Gophers are small, round animals. They have very small eyes and ears. Their bodies are covered with brown fur, but their tails are nearly bare. A prairie dog is a small, short-tailed animal. Like the gopher, it has small ears and eyes.

Gopher

Prairie dog eating grass

The prairie dog has lighter brown fur than the gopher and a much shorter tail. Prairie dogs get their unusual name from the barking sound they make. Gophers and prairie dogs both eat grasses and other tender plants. They help keep the soil healthy and loose. Gophers and prairie dogs are food for animals such as hawks, owls, and foxes.

Prairie dog

Let's **Think** About...

What does the heading on page 114 tell about the topic of burrowing animals?
Expository Text

115

Gopher and prairie dog burrows are not the same. A gopher burrow can be 100 feet long or more. Gophers also build 6–12 mounds in their burrows. The mounds let them go in and out when they need to. Gopher mounds are very well hidden. Covers on the mounds keep the burrows dark and keep other animals out.

Prairie dog mound

Prairie dog mounds are large and easy to see. They leave their mounds open. The holes in the mounds let them watch for animals that may be hunting them. Prairie dogs also like wind and light coming into their burrows.

Burrowing Owls

Sometimes we are surprised at the creatures that burrow. Burrowing owls live in prairie dog or gopher burrows.

Let's Think About...

What is the most important idea of these two paragraphs?
Expository Text

Burrowing owl

But if an owl can't find a ready-made burrow, it will scratch out one of its own.

Burrowing owls are smaller than most other owls. They may be only 10 inches tall and weigh less than half a pound. These birds have brown and black spots on their feathers and long legs.

Burrowing owls

Most owls hunt only at night. But during the day, burrowing owls hunt for insects. To make catching insects easier, the owls gather animal droppings. They put the droppings around the opening of their burrows. The droppings attract bugs. Then the owls can easily catch bugs to eat. Then at night they hunt for small animals.

Let's Think About...

Reading Across Texts *Soil* gives lots of facts. Which of these facts would be important for a burrowing animal?

Writing Across Texts Write a paragraph telling how soil facts are important to a burrowing animal.

Common Core State Standards

Foundational Skills 4.b. Read on-level text orally with accuracy, appropriate rate, and expression on successive readings. **Also Foundational Skills 3.d., Speaking/Listening 4., Language 4.c.**

Let's Learn It!

**READING STREET ONLINE
ONLINE STUDENT EDITION
www.ReadingStreet.com**

Get Ready For Grade 3

Use appropriate voice level and pace when you speak.

Listening and Speaking

Speak Well

You should always speak clearly and carefully. Use complete sentences. Speak at an appropriate pace. Do not talk too fast or too slow. Use an appropriate voice level. Make sure your voice is not too loud or too soft. Look at the people you are talking to.

Practice It! Tell the class about a game you like to play. Explain and share why you like to play the game.

Tips

- Use conventions of language when you speak.

- Use present tense verbs to describe what you do in the game.

118

Vocabulary

Suffixes

Word Structure A **suffix** is a word part added to the end of a word. You can use these suffixes to help you determine the meaning of the words.

fear   fearless
The suffix **-less** means "without," so **fearless** means "without fear."

Practice It! Determine the meaning of each bold word. Use the meaning of the suffix to help you.

1. I thought the banging would never stop. It seemed **endless**.
2. Baby mice are born **hairless**.
3. The team members were **joyless** when they lost the game.

Fluency

Read with Appropriate Phrasing

When you read, try to read words in groups. Do not read word-by-word. This way you understand what you read.

Practice It! Read the sentences aloud.

1. The park is at the end of this street.
2. The children finished their chores and went outside to play.
3. It's nice today, so I will go to the park.

Oral Vocabulary

Let's Talk About

Difficult Changes

- Share information about why it is difficult to live in a new place.

- Share ideas about why it is difficult to grow older.

READING STREET ONLINE
CONCEPT TALK VIDEO
www.ReadingStreet.com

121

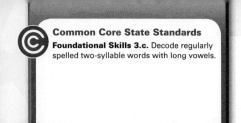

oatmeal

syllable pattern

tiger

V/CV

basket

VCCV

Phonics

Syllable Patterns

Words I Can Blend

boyhood

robot

oatmeal

picnic

tiger

Sentences I Can Read

1. In boyhood, boys sometimes pretend to be robots.

2. We ate oatmeal muffins at my picnic yesterday.

3. Did he see that new tiger yet?

I Can Read!

I think up super plans about how things can work better outdoors. It's kind of a hobby with me. I tell my plans to Mom and Dad. Once they believed I might explain my plan for saving raindrops with an expert. "Super!" I thought, until it was time to speak with him. All of a sudden I forgot what I was going to say. I was confused and upset.

Mom said quietly, "Relax, don't panic. Pretend we are just speaking with each other." It worked! And that man liked my plan.

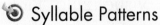
123

Common Core State Standards
Literature 2. Recount stories, including fables and folktales from diverse cultures, and determine their central message, lesson, or moral. **Also Literature 5., 7.**

Envision It! | Skill Strategy

Skill

Strategy

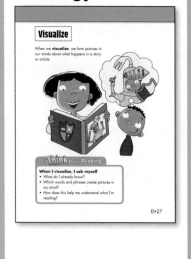

READING STREET ONLINE
ENVISION IT! ANIMATIONS
www.ReadingStreet.com

Comprehension Skill

🎯 Plot and Theme

- The plot is what happens at the beginning, middle, and end of a story.

- A story's theme is "the big idea" that the author wants the reader to learn from the story. This can be a moral lesson.

- Use what you learned about identifying plot and theme and fill out a chart like the one below as you read "The Space Flight."

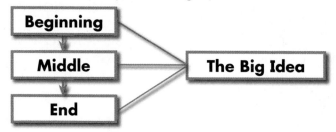

Comprehension Strategy

🎯 Visualize

Good readers picture how something looks, sounds, feels, tastes, or smells when they read. This is called visualizing. Picturing these details can help you monitor and adjust as you read. It also makes reading more fun.

The Space Flight

Maria brought a huge box in from the garage. She cut a square hole on one side.

"What's that?" Pedro asked.

"It's a window on our spaceship."

Maria and Pedro added buttons for the controls. Then they colored the side of the ship. Soon both kids were inside the box.

"Ready for take-off, Astronaut Pedro?"

"Ready!"

Maria counted down. Both kids shook the box back and forth as the ship took off. "Look over there, Pedro. Look how big the moon is!"

Pedro looked out the window. He did not see the sofa or the curtains. He saw outer space. "You're right. It's amazing!"

"See? With your imagination, you can go anywhere."

Strategy What do you see? How does this help you monitor and adjust your understanding?

Skill What is the theme of this story? What lesson could be learned?

Your Turn!

⏸ **Need a Review?** See the *Envision It! Handbook* for additional help with plot and theme and visualizing.

▷ **Ready to Try It?** As you read *The Night the Moon Fell*, use what you've learned to understand the text.

Envision It! | Words to Know

balance

canyons

coral

rattle

slivers

sway

whisper

READING STREET ONLINE
VOCABULARY ACTIVITIES
www.ReadingStreet.com

Vocabulary Strategy for

🎯 Multiple-Meaning Words

Context Clues During reading, you may come across a word you know, but the meaning doesn't fit in the sentence. The word may have more than one meaning. You can use the context clues to figure out its relevant meaning.

1. Try the meaning you know. Does it make sense? If not, the word may have more than one meaning.

2. Read on and look at the nearby words. Can you figure out another meaning?

3. Try the new meaning in the sentence. Does it make sense?

Read "Oak Creek Canyon." Use context clues to find the relevant meaning of the multiple-meaning words.

Words to Write Reread "Oak Creek Canyon." Where is your favorite place to walk? What do you see when you walk there? Use words from the *Words to Know* list.

Oak Creek Canyon

Nature has many great things to see. Fish and coral fill the sea. Mountains stretch up high to the sky. Tall grasses sway over miles of flat land. Deep canyons dig into the land. Oak Creek Canyon is one of these canyons.

Oak Creek Canyon has rocks with strange shapes. Over time, wind and water wore away slivers and chips of rocks. This gave them their shapes.

Visit the canyon in early morning. You can watch the sun come up. You can see light hit the rocks. It is a good time to explore! Walk carefully. You want to keep your balance as you explore.

Stop and listen. Do you hear the wind whisper through the tall trees? Do you hear something rattle? It may be a rattlesnake. You want to stay far away from it. Look around. Lizards live here too. The canyon is filled with sights and sounds, and it is not very cold. You will have a good time here.

Your Turn!

⏸ **Need a Review?** For more help with context clues and multiple-meaning words, see *Words!* on pp. W•7 and W•10.

▶ **Ready to Try It?** Read *The Night the Moon Fell* on pp. 128–143.

The Night

the Moon Fell

Question of the Week
Why are some changes difficult?

A Mayan myth retold by
Pat Mora

illustrated by
Domi

One night long ago, Luna the moon hummed high in the night sky. Stars twinkled, and Luna's friend the wind dozed nearby. The night was hushed and peaceful.

Suddenly, the sky shook. A loud **WHOOSH!** rattled the stars and startled the moon. Luna's grandfather had shot his blowgun, and Luna jumped in surprise. She lost her balance and started to roll and roll.

Luna rolled through stars, and she rolled through clouds. She rolled, rolled down to the earth and splashed into the ocean's cold, dark waves. She broke into shimmering slivers and bits on the sandy bottom of the sea.

The huge sky became black and still as the deepest ocean. Stars shut their eyes. Flowers bowed their heads, and all the birds in the world rose looking for the moon. They flew into loud storms. They soared down black canyons. They darted into huge caves calling,

"Luna, come back, bring us your light.
Shine your white light for us tonight."
Silence.
Luna's amigo, the wind, raced up mountains whispering and then roaring,
"Luna, come back, bring us your light.
Shine your white light for us tonight."
All the world waited. All the world listened.
Silence.

Where was the moon?

The tiny fish at the bottom of the sea knew. They saw Luna's white glow, and they heard her lonely song.

"Where am I? Where's the sky?
Broken, sad, lost am I."

The fish swam around and around the broken moon. "What can we do? What can we do?" they whispered.

"We'll be your friends," said the tiniest fish. "What's your name?"

"Luna," the moon sniffled.

"Are you the shining light that hums high in the sky?" asked the roundest fish.

Luna sniffed,

"I was the light high in the sky,
Now broken, sad, lost am I."

The tiny fish and Luna looked up together. They looked up through all that deep, dark water. The little fish missed seeing the moonlight high in the night sky. They missed playing in Luna's white light.

In a sad voice, Luna sighed,
"Oh, sweet fish, how sad am I.
I miss my home high in the sky."

The little fish felt sorry for Luna. "Watch this," said the tiniest fish, and he and the other little fish began blowing bubbles in wonderful and funny shapes to make her laugh and smile.

"New friends, you are good for me.
You make me laugh in this cold, dark sea."

The tiny fish began to hum, and in time Luna hummed too. She hummed herself to sleep.

When she woke, Luna looked around.
She saw colors! She saw forests of coral and kelp,
gold fish that glistened and blue fish that flew. Sea
horses galloped gently by, and starfish waved their
lavender arms.

"Yes," said the roundest fish. "Our water
world is beautiful too."

"Ooooohhhh!" said Luna, gasping at all
the spinning, silver whirls, and her surprised,
"Ooooohhhhh!" rose into glowing bubbles.

But a large, dark shape with eyes cold as stones brushed by. Bright fish darted away. Luna stopped smiling and rolled into a nearby cave.

"He's gone now, Luna," called the roundest fish. "High or low, there is danger, but I know you are clever and brave."

"Am I?" asked Luna, but deep inside she knew she was. She said, "I tell my friend the wind,

'All you need is part of you,
Ask yourself what you should do.' "

The roundest fish said, "Luna, ask yourself what you should do, and we'll help."

"Let me think," said Luna. She thought and she thought, and the tiny fish hummed softly to help her thinking.

Luna started swaying to their music, and the fish swayed with her. Then Luna began to hum and to roll to her music, and as she rolled in the strange new land, she began to collect herself.

"How can we help?" asked the tiniest fish.

Luna sang,

"All you need is part of you.

Ask yourself what you should do."

The tiny fish thought and thought. They whispered, ***"Pppzzz, pppzzz. Pppzzz, pppzzz."*** And then they knew what to do. The little fish looked inside shells and deep in cold sea caves for bits of glowing moon. With their silvery fins, they began to sweep together the slivers and bits, and on the strange sand, the moon rolled and rolled into herself.

She said,
"Pezecitos,
little fish,
    Smooth me
whole. Please
grant my wish."
    The fish swam
round-round
Luna, patching and
smoothing.
With their silvery fins,
they smoothed her roundness.
Luna laughed at the tickly fins. When she
studied herself, Luna knew she needed just
a bit of her friends to stay together, so she said,
    "Now what I need is part of you.
    Will you be my silvery glue?"

137

The little fish looked at themselves.
The tiny fish thought and thought.
They whispered, *"Pppzzz, pppzzz,
pppzzz."* Luna smiled and hummed.
The fish began to wriggle and dance.
And they knew what to do. They shook
themselves to loosen a few of their
silvery scales, and with their fins they
patched the rolling moon. As Luna
rolled into herself, the sea around her
glistened. Luna began to hum and
glow.

Oh, how beautiful she looked when
she was round and whole again! The
deep ocean was filled with her white
light. Waves rolled rainbows. The little
fish rested.

Luna then said,
"Gracias, mis amigos, thank you.
Thank you for your silvery glue."

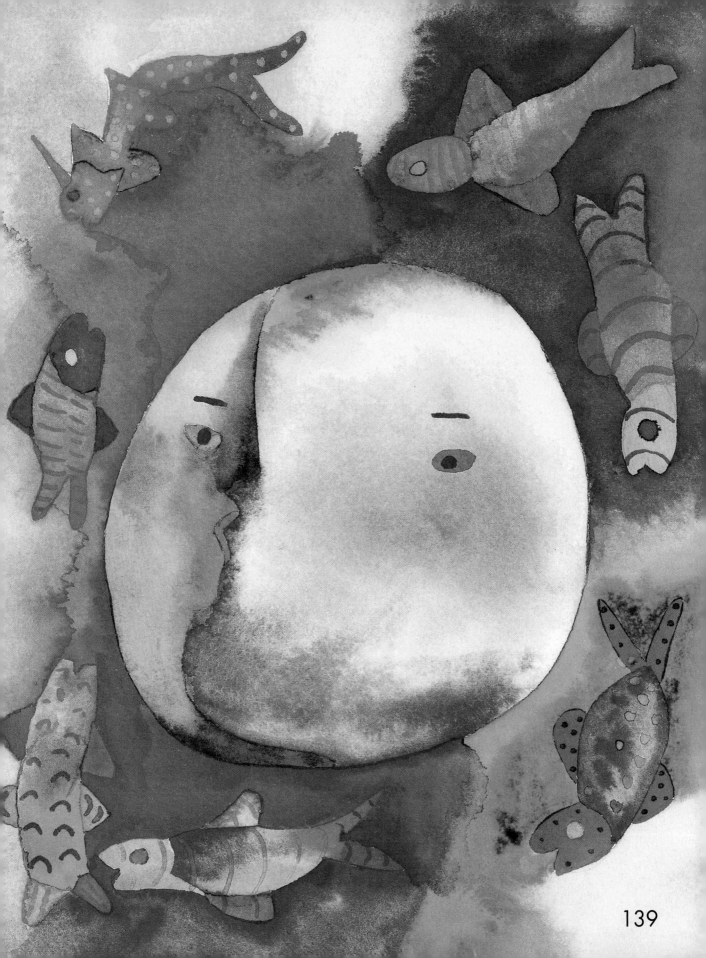

"You're so happy, you're like a balloon," said the littlest fish, watching the moon begin to float.

Luna laughed,

"Now round and whole am I,

And can float home to my sky."

The fish watched Luna float slowly up from the bottom of the sea. They whispered,

"Pppzzz, pppzzz. Pppzzz, pppzzz."

And then they knew what to do.
Holding on to one another's tails, the
tiny fish wove themselves into a silvery
net around Luna.

"That tickles, friends,
but I agree.

Come swim the sky. Accompany me."

Slowly, Luna and the tiny fish rose through
the clouds and through the stars. When they
were high in the night sky, Luna began to hum,
and the night sky changed. Luna's white light
opened the stars' eyes, and her friend the wind
purred. Flowers lifted their heads, and birds
flew high, sang one note, and then nestled in
trees and on rooftops.

The moon was home, and she sang new songs of gold fish and starfish, of coral and kelp, of rolling rainbow waves.

Luna's friends, the tiny fish, started swimming in the huge night sky. They heard her voice, sweeter than the scent of a thousand flowers, softer than the *ssshhh, ssshhh, ssshhh* of waves at dawn.

Luna sang,
"Please, dear friends, stay here with me.
Swim my skies, my star bright sea."
And they did.
Look up. High in the sky, Luna's friend
the wind dozes, and her amigos, the tiny
fish, swim nearby. They twinkle through the
night, and Luna smiles her white light.

143

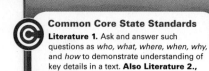

Think Critically

1. What does the moon look like in the sky? How does it change? **Text to World**

2. Why do you think the author retells this myth? What lesson does the author want to teach? **Think Like an Author**

3. What happens when Luna returns to the sky at the end of the myth? **Plot and Theme**

4. Tell what you see when you read about Luna falling from the sky to the sea. **Visualize**

5. **Look Back and Write** Look back at pages 136–138. What do the little fish do to help Luna return to the sky? Provide evidence to support your answer.

    Key Ideas and Details • Text Evidence

Meet the Illustrator

Domi

Domi is a Mazatec Indian from Mexico. She uses many native traditions in her art.

At a young age, she watched her aunts weave native clothing. At night, she practiced on her own, creating brightly colored patterns. When she was 20, she first tried painting. She painted colorful figures on a wall in her living room.

Domi feels that art is extremely important in our day-to-day lives. "You must paint, dance, do something creative so that you can stay healthy."

Read two more books illustrated by Domi.

Napí Goes to the Mountain

The Race of Toad and Deer

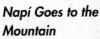

Use the *Reader's and Writer's Notebook* to record your independent reading.

Common Core State Standards
Writing 3. Write narratives in which they recount a well-elaborated event or short sequence of events, include details to describe actions, thoughts, and feelings, use temporal words to signal event order, and provide a sense of closure.
Also Language 1.e., 6.

Let's Write It!

Key Features of a Narrative Poem

- tells a story
- may have rhyming words
- can describe something or can express feelings

READING STREET ONLINE
GRAMMAR JAMMER
www.ReadingStreet.com

Narrative

Narrative Poem

A **narrative poem** tells a story. Poems can be read aloud. They often have words that rhyme. The student model on the next page is an example of a narrative poem.

Writing Prompt Think about a change that has happened in your life. Now write a poem about it.

Writer's Checklist

Remember, you should . . .

☑ tell a story in your poem.

☑ use your own writer's voice to show your memory or feelings.

☑ say and hear your poem.

☑ use adverbs that tell when and where.

Wait and See

Jake came home yesterday.

Our baby cannot walk or play.

Mama carried him here.

She fed him. She called him "dear."

Mama says just wait and see.

Jake will grow up like me.

First he'll walk, and then he'll run.

He and I will have so much fun.

Adverbs can tell when or where. Words such as *first* and *then* show the order of events.

Writing Trait Voice
The writer's feeling about fun in the future is clear.

Genre
A **narrative poem** tells a story.

Conventions

- ## Adverbs That Tell When and Where

  Remember Adverbs tell more about verbs. Some adverbs tell **when** or **where**. I had lunch **before**.

- **Time-order words** such as **first, then,** and **next** help show the order in which things happen.

147

Common Core State Standards
Informational Text 5. Know and use various text features (e.g., captions, bold print, subheadings, glossaries, indexes, electronic menus, icons) to locate key facts or information in a text efficiently.

21st Century Skills
INTERNET GUY

E-mail is great! E-mail other students around the world. Work on a project together. Make our world a better place. Or, read a good book together. Then share your ideas by e-mail.

- E-mail is short for "electronic mail." It can be sent over the Internet from one computer to another.

- An e-mail can be used to communicate with family and friends.

- An e-mail is like a friendly letter.

- Read "A New House." Use the pictures and the text to learn how e-mail works.

A New House

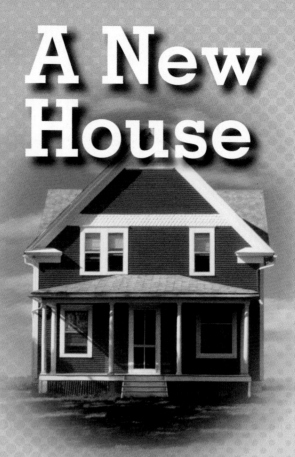

Moving to a new home can be difficult but exciting. Writing an e-mail message can help you keep in touch with family and friends far away. Here is how e-mail works.

When you turn on your computer and go into your e-mail, you can do these things:

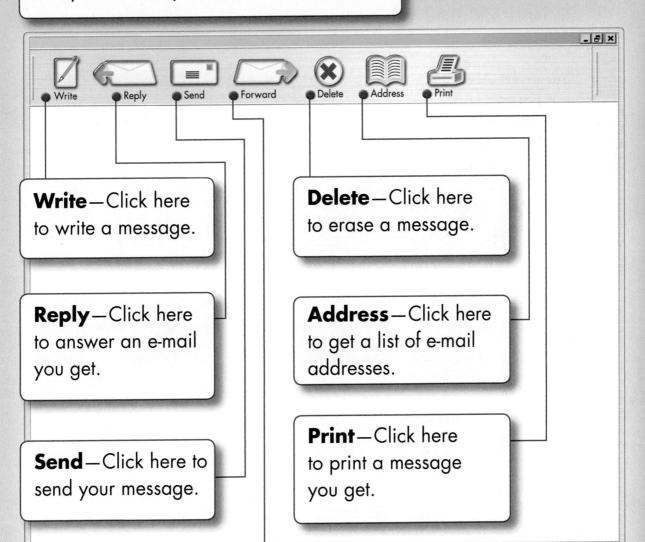

Write—Click here to write a message.

Reply—Click here to answer an e-mail you get.

Send—Click here to send your message.

Forward—Click here to send a message you get to someone else.

Delete—Click here to erase a message.

Address—Click here to get a list of e-mail addresses.

Print—Click here to print a message you get.

149

How to Send E-mail

To write and send an e-mail, you need a person's e-mail address. E-mail addresses look like this:

(name of person)@(where message is going)

The letters on the left name the person or place you are writing to. People often use nicknames or abbreviations. The symbol @ stands for the word *at*. The letters to the right of the @ sign tell where in the world the message is going.

To write an e-mail, you click on a button that says **Write** or **Compose** or **New**. A new window will open that looks something like this:

To: You type the receiver's name here.

Subject: You type the subject of your message here. It is always best to fill this in.

Now you are ready to type your message, like the one on the next page.

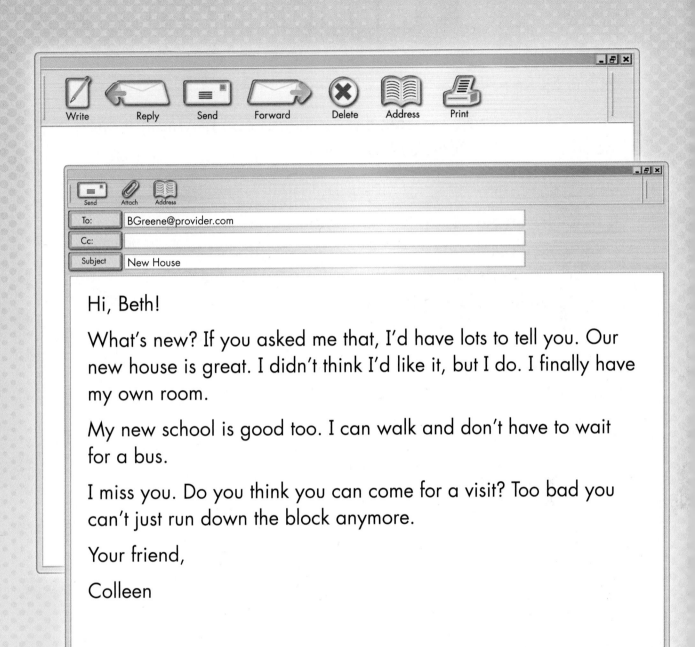

Write   Reply   Send   Forward   Delete   Address   Print

Send   Attach   Address

To: BGreene@provider.com

Cc:

Subject   New House

Hi, Beth!

What's new? If you asked me that, I'd have lots to tell you. Our new house is great. I didn't think I'd like it, but I do. I finally have my own room.

My new school is good too. I can walk and don't have to wait for a bus.

I miss you. Do you think you can come for a visit? Too bad you can't just run down the block anymore.

Your friend,

Colleen

Common Core State Standards
Foundational Skills 4.a. Read on-level text with purpose and understanding. **Also Informational Text 7., Speaking/Listening 1.a., Language 4.**

Let's **Learn** It!

Describe how media may use graphics to tell facts and opinions.

Media Literacy

Describe Media Techniques

Media resources can give information or entertain. They may tell facts or opinions. They may use graphics, such as photographs, drawings, diagrams, and graphs. The graphics provide information too.

Practice It! Work in groups. Find an article on the Internet or in a magazine or newspaper. Study the article. Look at the graphics. What information do they give? Does the article include opinions as well as facts? Is there any misleading information? As a group, tell the class about your article. Remember to take turns and speak clearly.

Tips

- Describe how techniques, such as graphics, are used to create media messages.

- Describe how the graphics make a product or a story more interesting.

Vocabulary

Multiple-Meaning Words

Context Clues You may read a word that you know but the meaning does not seem to fit. The context clues will help you understand the word's relevant meaning.

Practice It! Read and write each sentence. Circle the meaning for each bold word.

1. You should not **skip** breakfast in the morning.

   hop   leave out

2. I cannot reach that high **note** when I sing.

   tone   reminder

Fluency

Read with Expression

Reading with expression makes a story more exciting. Reading as if the characters were speaking makes the story full of life and energy.

Practice It! Read the sentences aloud.

1. "Have you acted before?" the director asked.

2. "Can I please stay up five minutes longer?" Cal begged.

Oral Vocabulary

Let's Talk About

Changes in the Weather

- Share information about how weather can cause damage.

- Share ideas about how weather affects food supply.

READING STREET ONLINE
CONCEPT TALK VIDEO
www.ReadingStreet.com

154

155

Common Core State Standards
Foundational Skills 3.b. Know spelling-sound correspondences for additional common vowel teams.

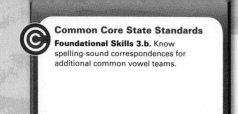

Envision It! | Sounds to Know

moon

oo

glue

ue

newt

ew

fruit

ui

**READING STREET ONLINE
SOUND-SPELLING CARDS**
www.ReadingStreet.com

Phonics

Vowel Digraphs *oo, ue, ew, ui*

Words I Can Blend

fruit
juice
honeydew
blueberries
bloomed

Sentences I Can Read

1. Which fruit juice does he like most?

2. Drew likes honeydew, but I like blueberries.

3. That plant grew big and then bloomed.

I Can Read!

Lewis has a new pool. Each day at noon he puts on his swimsuit, leaves his room, and jumps in the pool. Lewis believes it is true that working out in the pool is good for you. After his workout, Lewis drinks a cool glass of fruit juice. Last week, Lewis threw a pool party. There was gobs of good food, and Lewis made some new friends too. He's glad he has a pool.

You've learned

- Vowel Digraphs *oo, ue, ew, ui*

Common Core State Standards

Literature 1. Ask and answer such questions as *who, what, where, when, why,* and *how* to demonstrate understanding of key details in a text. **Also Literature 2., 5.**

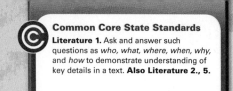

Envision It! | Skill Strategy

Skill

Strategy

READING STREET ONLINE
ENVISION IT! ANIMATIONS
www.ReadingStreet.com

Comprehension Skill

Plot and Theme

- A plot is what happens at the beginning, middle, and end of a story.

- A story's theme is the "big idea" that the author wants the reader to learn from the story. This can be a moral lesson.

- Use what you learned about identifying theme and plot and fill out an organizer like the one below as you read "The Grasshopper and the Ant."

Beginning	
Middle	
End	

Comprehension Strategy

Monitor and Clarify

Good readers make sure they understand what they read. Does something seem confusing to you as you read? Seek clarification. First, ask yourself a question. Then reread the paragraph. Think about what it says. Does it answer your question?

The Grasshopper and the Ant

Long ago, a grasshopper met an ant. The ant carried a piece of corn on her back.

The grasshopper said, "Hello! Would you like to sing with me?"

The ant said, "I have no time to sing. I have to get a lot of corn to my nest. I will need the food for winter."

"Why worry about winter?" asked the grasshopper. "Winter will not be here for a long time."

Strategy Did you read something you did not understand? Ask a question. Reread the text to find the answer.

"You won't have any food in the winter if you do not work now," said the ant. The grasshopper laughed at the ant.

Many months passed. Winter came. All the leaves were gone. Snow was all around. The grasshopper could not find food and was very hungry.

The ant was not hungry. She had plenty of corn to eat. The ant was ready for winter because she had prepared for it.

Skill What is the lesson to be learned? What is the theme of the story?

Your Turn!

 Need a Review? See the *Envision It! Handbook* for additional help with plot and theme and monitor and clarify.

▶ **Ready to Try It?** As you read *The First Tortilla*, use what you've learned to understand the text.

159

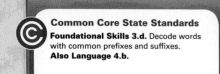

Common Core State Standards
Foundational Skills 3.d. Decode words with common prefixes and suffixes.
Also Language 4.b.

Vocabulary Strategy for

🎯 Prefixes

Word Structure When you read, you may come to a word you don't know. Look at the word. Does the word have the prefix *re-* or *dis-*? The prefix *re-* added to a word makes the word mean "____ again." The prefix *dis-* added to a word makes the word mean "not ____." Use these prefixes to help you figure out the meanings of words you don't know.

1. Put your finger over the prefix.

2. Look at the base word. Put the base word in the phrase "____ again" or "not ____."

3. Try that meaning in the sentence. Does it make sense?

Read "Hector and the Scarecrow." Use the prefixes to help you determine the meanings of the words.

Words to Write Reread "Hector and the Scarecrow." Write what you think happens next. Use words from the *Words to Know* list.

Envision It! | Words to Know

awaken

mountain

rainbow

cliffs

prize

suffer

volcano

Hector and the Scarecrow

Hector heard people tell and retell stories about the volcano near his home. They said that it was a scary place. They said everything there could talk, even the trees and rocks. Hector disagreed. He did not think it could be that scary, so he quietly left his home one morning. He did not want to awaken the other people in town. They would try to stop him if they were awake.

Hector climbed the volcano. He reached some cliffs near the top. Tall, green cornstalks grew on the cliffs. A single scarecrow stood nearby. The scarecrow wore a red coat, blue pants, and a yellow hat. "He looks like a rainbow. What a prize!" thought Hector. Then the scarecrow said, "Oh. Hello there." Hector was amazed! The scarecrow spoke, but it sounded sad.

Hector asked, "Is something wrong?"

The scarecrow said, "I dislike this place. I want to visit a different mountain."

Hector did not want to see the scarecrow suffer. He said, "Come home with me. We will sleep tonight. Tomorrow, I will help you find another mountain."

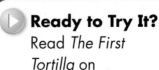

Your Turn!

▐▐ **Need a Review?** For more help with using prefixes to determine the meaning of a word, see *Words!* on p. W•5.

▶ **Ready to Try It?** Read *The First Tortilla* on pp. 162–176.

The First Tortilla

The First Tortilla

by Rudolfo Anaya
illustrated by Amy Córdova

Genre A **legend** is an old story that tells about the great deeds of a hero. Now read about how a young girl becomes a hero in her village.

162

How do changes in the weather affect us?

Jade opened her eyes and yawned. She knew she had slept late because the sun had already risen.

"Time to awaken, precious Jade," her mother whispered. She was crushing dry chile pods in a metate.

"Time to greet the sun," her father said. He was weaving a basket. Each day Jade's parents went to the village market to sell their colorful baskets.

Jade jumped out of the hammock and greeted her parents. After breakfast she hurried outside to water the garden.

A huge volcano towered over Jade's village. On the peak of the mountain lived the Mountain Spirit. When the Mountain Spirit spoke, the earth rumbled and smoke filled the sky. Sometimes burning lava poured down the mountainside. Jade said a prayer. "Mountain Spirit, send us rain. Our bean and squash plants are dying."

She picked up a clay pot and walked to the lake. Jade greeted the other village girls who were also collecting water. The once beautiful lake was almost dry. She filled the pot and returned to the garden. As she worked a lovely blue hummingbird flew in front of her.

"You must go to the Mountain Spirit and ask for rain," the hummingbird whispered. "And you must take a gift."

Her father had told her the small birds brought messages from the Mountain Spirit. Jade knew she must listen.

"The path is very dangerous," she said.

"I will guide you," the hummingbird replied.

Jade ran back into the hut.

"What is it, my daughter?" her mother asked.

Jade told her parents what had happened.

Her mother smiled and said, "A blue hummingbird flew over your crib when you were born. It was a special sign."

"Why don't the rains come?" Jade asked her father.

"Years ago we had rain and good harvests, but the people forgot to thank the Mountain Spirit. We did not take gifts to the mountain. Now it is angry, and there is no rain."

"I can take a gift of food," Jade said.

Her father shook his head. "A girl cannot climb the mountain. You will fall from the cliffs like a bird without wings."

"Our gardens are dying," her mother said. "Soon we must leave our home in search of food. That will be the end of our way of life."

Jade grew sad. She knew the people did not want to leave their village. They had lived at the foot of the volcano for many generations. This had been the home of their ancestors.

When her parents were gone to market, Jade walked in the garden, wondering what she could do to help her village.

The blue hummingbird appeared again.

"The Mountain Spirit will listen to you," the hummingbird whispered.

"Can I do it?" Jade asked.

Her father had said that she might fall from the cliff like a bird without wings. But if she didn't go the entire village would suffer.

"Yes, I will go," she decided.

She warmed a bowl of beans and squash and sprinkled chile powder on the food.

"I hope this pleases the Mountain Spirit," she said.

She gathered a *rebozo* around her shoulders and followed the hummingbird up the narrow path. Suddenly the mountain shook and boulders came crashing down.

"This way!" the hummingbird cried.

Jade jumped aside, and the boulders missed her.

Finally they arrived at the home of the Mountain Spirit, where butterflies danced among a rainbow of flowers. A waterfall cascaded into a clear, blue lake.

"Why have you come?" the Mountain Spirit asked. Thunder and smoke filled the sky.

"I came to ask for rain," Jade replied. "Without rain our plants will die and we will starve."

"Your people no longer honor me!" the Mountain Spirit said.

"I have not forgotten you," Jade answered. "I brought you a gift."

She uncovered the bowl of beans and squash. A pleasant aroma filled the air,
The Mountain Spirit was pleased.

"You are a brave girl. I will send rain. And I will give you a gift. You may have the food the ants store in the cave."

Jade looked at the ants scurrying on the ground.
"The ants carry pebbles," Jade said.
"Look closely," the Mountain Spirit whispered.
Jade fell on her knees.
"What are you carrying?" she asked the ants.
"This is corn," one ant replied.
"Taste it," another ant said, offering a kernel.
Jade chewed the corn. "Oh, what a sweet flavor!" she cried. "Where does it come from?"

171

"It grows here on Corn Mountain. We gather the grains and store them in a cave. Come with us."

Jade followed the ants into the cavern. On the floor she found piles of corn.

"Corn is a gift from the Mountain Spirit," the ant said. "Take all you want."

Jade gathered the corn in her rebozo. She thanked the Mountain Spirit. She thanked the

hummingbird for guiding her. And she thanked the ants for sharing their corn.

Then she carefully made her way down the mountain with her prize. Her parents had returned from the market. Jade entered her home and spilled the corn on the floor.

"What is this?" her father asked.

"Corn!" Jade cried. "The Mountain Spirit gave it to me. Here, taste it!"

Her father chewed a few dry kernels, and the corn softened with each bite. It was sweet and tasty.

"Good," said her father. "But hard to chew."

"I will boil the corn in a clay pot," said her mother. "It will make pozol."

When the *pozol* was ready, Jade's father tasted it.

"Wonderful!" he exclaimed. "We must thank the Mountain Spirit for this food."

They scattered kernels of corn in their garden and said a prayer of thanks.

That afternoon clouds gathered on the mountain peak. Soon a gentle rain fell. Later in the season corn plants pushed through the earth.

The corn tassels blossomed. Soon tender ears of corn appeared on the stalks.

"*Elotes*," Jade said as she picked the corn. That evening they ate corn, beans, and squash flavored with red chile.

When the corn was dry Jade placed some kernels in a *metate* and crushed them with a *mano*. She sprinkled water on the cornmeal.

The gruel was thick, like dough.

"*Masa*," Jade said. She patted the masa back and forth in her palms until it was flat and round. Then she placed it on a hot stone near the fire.

While they were eating they smelled the masa cooking on the hot stone.

"What is that sweet aroma?" asked her father.

"The masa!" Jade cried.

There on the hot stone lay the freshly baked bread. She picked it up and offered it to her parents.

Her father ate a piece. "Hum, very good!"

"Delicious!" her mother exclaimed. "What shall we call this bread?"

Jade thought a while. "I'll call it a *tortilla*."

"I am proud of you," her father said.

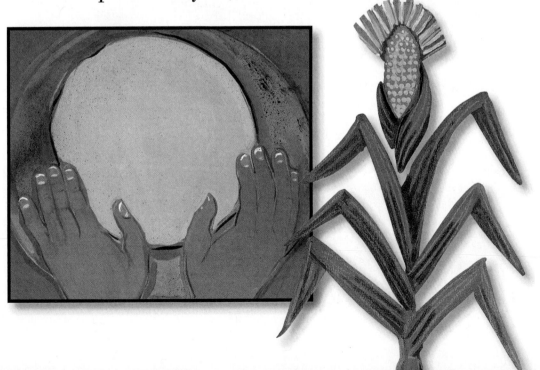

"We must share this with our neighbors," her mother added.

In the following days Jade went from home to home, teaching the women how to make tortillas.

The corn plants grew. Corn tortillas became the favorite food of the people. Now the villagers did not have to leave their home.

During the harvest fiesta the people held a ceremony to thank the Mountain Spirit for giving them corn. They also thanked Jade, the girl who had baked the first tortilla.

Corn Tortilla Recipe

Tortillas are the bread of Mexico. They are used for classic Tex-Mex dishes like tacos and tostados. Have an adult help you try this tasty recipe at home.

Ingredients

- 2 cups masa harina (a traditional corn flour)
- 1 tsp sea salt
- ¼ tsp baking soda
- 2 cups very warm water
- 1 tsp oil

In a large bowl, mix corn flour, salt, baking soda, warm water, and oil.

Stir until dough stays together and does not break apart. Knead until dough forms a large ball. It should be soft and not sticky. Cover and let stand for two minutes.

Pull off balls of dough, and roll each one into a flat, thin circle.

Have an adult heat a heavy iron pan.

Have an adult cook the tortillas until both sides are golden brown.

Eat with meat filling, shredded cheese, or plain.

Makes about 12 tortillas

Glossary

jade	a precious stone in ancient Mexico
rebozo	a shawl worn by Mexican women
pozol	or posole, a corn and meat stew
elote	*elotl,* an ancient Mexican word for ear of corn
metate	concave rock where corn is ground
mano	smooth rock with which to grind corn
masa	dough
tortilla	traditional Mexican bread

Common Core State Standards

Literature 1. Ask and answer such questions as *who, what, where, when, why,* and *how* to demonstrate understanding of key details in a text. **Also Literature 2., Writing 1.**

Envision It! Retell

READING STREET ONLINE
STORY SORT
www.ReadingStreet.com

Think Critically

1. Tortillas became the favorite food of the villagers. What are your favorite foods? **Text to Self**

2. Why does the author tell a legend about how the first tortilla was made from corn? What lesson does the author want to teach? **Think Like an Author**

3. What do the villagers learn by the end of the story? **Plot and Theme**

4. Reread the tortilla recipe on page 177. What steps does an adult need to do? Why is that important? **Monitor and Clarify**

5. **Look Back and Write** Look back at page 169. Do you think Jade is brave? Provide evidence to support your answer.

   Key Ideas and Details • Text Evidence

Rudolfo Anaya

Rudolfo Anaya leads an active life, wanting "to do more." He has visited many places. He has fished and climbed mountains. He has been a college professor and is an author of books for children and adults.

Amy Córdova

Amy Córdova lives in the mountains of New Mexico. She has illustrated several children's books and also writes stories. She says, "When I draw, my pictures tell stories. Through my writing, I make pictures."

Read more books written by Rudolfo Anaya or illustrated by Amy Córdova.

Roadrunner's Dance

Dream Carver

Use the *Reader's and Writer's Notebook* to record your independent reading.

Common Core State Standards

Writing 3. Write narratives in which they recount a well-elaborated event or short sequence of events, include details to describe actions, thoughts, and feelings, use temporal words to signal event order, and provide a sense of closure. **Also Language 1.e., 2., 6.**

Let's Write It!

Key Features of a Thank-You Note

- thanks someone
- is a short message
- has a date, greeting, and closing

READING STREET ONLINE
GRAMMAR JAMMER
www.ReadingStreet.com

Thank-You Note

Thank-You Note

A **thank-you note** thanks someone for something they did. It is a kind of short friendly letter. The student model on the next page is an example of a thank-you note.

Writing Prompt Think about how thankful people are for food during any season. Write a thank-you note to someone who has prepared food for you.

Writer's Checklist

Remember, you should . . .

☑ tell the person why you are thankful.

☑ use capital letters in the date, greeting, and closing.

☑ use adverbs that tell how.

May 10, 2011

Dear Aunt Maria,

Today you gave me some of your special salsa. I saw you carefully chop tomatoes, peppers, and onions.

Thank you for mixing the delicious salsa and giving me some.

Two friends ate dinner at my house. We put the salsa on our tacos. It was gone quickly. Everyone liked it.

Love,

Lamar

Writing Trait Focus
The writer focuses on the reason for writing.

The writer uses **adverbs** that tell how.

Genre Thank-you notes express thanks and have a date, greeting, and closing.

Conventions

Adverbs That Tell How

Remember An **adverb** tells more about a verb. Adverbs that tell how may end with the letters **-ly.**

quickly   carefully   beautifully

181

Common Core State Standards
Informational Text 2. Identify the main topic of a multiparagraph text as well as the focus of specific paragraphs within the text. Also Informational Text 5., 6.

Wind

by Marion Dane Bauer

Genre
Expository Text

- Expository text explains an animal, place, thing, or idea.

- Expository text gives facts and details.

- Expository text often has graphic features such as pictures and diagrams.

- Text features such as captions often go with graphic features. Captions give specific information.

- Read "Wind." Look for elements of expository text in this selection.

The Earth we live on is a spinning ball. When Earth spins, the air around it moves too.

When air moves, we call it "wind." As the sun heats the air, the air grows lighter. Light air rises.

Let's **Think** About...

What facts do you learn about hot and cool air on this page? **Expository Text**

Cool air is heavy. It falls. Cool air and warm air are always trading places. We call this movement "wind."

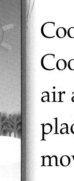

Let's **Think** About...

To what living things is wind important? **Expository Text**

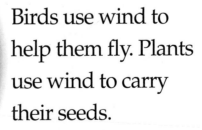

Birds use wind to help them fly. Plants use wind to carry their seeds.

We use wind to fly kites, to sail boats, and to turn windmills.

Let's Think About...

What are some different ways that people use wind? **Expository Text**

Wind moves clouds. Wind makes waves. It even makes trees bend. When the hot air is very light and the cold air is very heavy, wind can blow up a storm!

Sometimes wind spins like a puppy chasing its tail. A small spin makes a dust devil or a water spout. A strong spin makes a tornado or a hurricane.

dust devil

view of hurricane from space

tornado

Wind can be scary. Or it can sing a gentle song. Wind is all around us, but we cannot see it. We can only see what wind does.

Let's Think About...

Reading Across Texts What wind characteristics did the Mountain Spirit from *The First Tortilla* have?

Writing Across Texts Write a paragraph explaining your answer.

185

Common Core State Standards
Foundational Skills 3.d. Decode words with common prefixes and suffixes. **Also Foundational Skills 4.b., Speaking/Listening 2., Language 4.b.**

Vocabulary

Prefixes

Word Structure A prefix is a word part added to the beginning of a word. You can use the prefix to determine the meaning of a word.

Remember, the prefix *dis-* often means "not," and the prefix *re-* often means "again."

Practice It! Read and write each word. Use the prefixes to determine the meanings, and then write them down.

**disagree   disloyal
reawaken   rewrite**

Fluency

Expression and Intonation

When reading aloud, make your voice sound like you are talking. Raise your voice at the end of questions. Show strong feelings when reading an exclamation.

Practice It! Read each set of sentences using expression and intonation.

1. Everyone wondered what would happen next. Would the mystery be solved?

2. The sky is cloudy and dark. Do you think it will rain?

Listening and Speaking

Get Ready For Grade 3

Retell the important ideas when you summarize.

Give an Oral Summary

When you summarize a story, you retell it in your own words. You retell only the most important parts. You retell the parts in order. Speak clearly and slowly so others can understand you.

Practice It! Choose one of the stories you have read. Work with a friend to summarize the story. Use descriptive words to help make your summary interesting. Present your summary to the class. Take turns and speak clearly. Be polite when your partner is summarizing part of the story. Listen and do not interrupt.

Tips

• Remember a summary is shorter than the story. The summary tells just the important ideas.

• Use time-order transition words in your summary to retell the story in sequence.

What does it mean to be responsible?

Responsibility

U.S. COAST GUARD

255018

Common Core State Standards

Language 6. Use words and phrases acquired through conversations, reading and being read to, and responding to texts, including using adjectives and adverbs to describe (e.g., *When other kids are happy that makes me happy*).
Also Speaking/Listening 1.

Let's Talk About

Responsibility

● Share information about communicating with and helping each other.

● Share ideas about respecting each other.

READING STREET ONLINE
CONCEPT TALK VIDEO
www.ReadingStreet.com

191

Common Core State Standards
Foundational Skills 3.d. Decode words with common prefixes and suffixes.
Also Language 4.c.

Envision It! | Words to Know

burning

masks

station

building

quickly

roar

tightly

READING STREET ONLINE
VOCABULARY ACTIVITIES
www.ReadingStreet.com

Vocabulary Strategy for

🎯 Suffix -*ly*

Word Structure When you read, you may come to a word you don't know. You might look for a suffix. Does the word have -*ly* at the end? When the suffix -*ly* is added to a word, it usually makes the word mean "in a ____ way." For example, *kindly* means "in a kind way."

1. Put your finger over the -*ly* suffix.

2. Look at the base word. Put the base word in the phrase "in a ____ way."

3. Try that meaning in the sentence. Does it make sense?

Read "A Trip to the Fire Station." Look for words that end with -*ly*. Use the suffix to help you determine the meanings of the words.

Words to Write Reread "A Trip to the Fire Station." What might happen to Carlos next? Write a story about what might happen. Use words from the *Words to Know* list.

A TRIP TO
THE FIRE STATION

Carlos is a firefighter. Some children are at his fire station for a tour. He points out where the firefighters sleep and eat. Carlos slides down the fire pole. "That is how we quickly get from our beds to the trucks," he says.

"We use hoses to spray water on a fire," he says. "Fire hoses can be very heavy when they are filled with water. We have to grip the hoses tightly."

"Fires give off a lot of smoke," Carlos tells the children. "We must wear air tanks and masks if we go into a fire. We use masks to breathe clean air."

Carlos shows the children his thick clothes, heavy boots, and hard helmet. "These keep me safe from the things that can fall from or in a burning building."

Suddenly, the fire alarm goes off! Carlos tells the children good-bye. He puts on his gear and climbs onto the fire truck. With a loud roar, the fire truck races off.

Your Turn!

❚❚ **Need a Review?** For more help with using suffixes to determine the meanings of words, see *Words!* on p. W•6.

Let's Think About..

▶ **Ready to Try It?**
Read *Fire Fighter!* on pp. 198–211.

Genre

Literary nonfiction
tells about a true event or a
series of events like a story.
Look for true events in the
day of a firefighter.

Fire Fighter!

by Angela Royston

Question of the Week

Why should we be responsible for doing a good job?

Let's Think About Reading!

It is busy at the fire station even when there is no fire. Liz is checking the hoses. She wants to make sure they screw tightly to the truck.

Dan is polishing the fire truck wheels. Anthony is upstairs in the kitchen, looking for a snack. He is always hungry! Suddenly a loud noise makes him jump.

Let's Think About...

What do you think will happen next? What makes you think that? Read on to confirm your prediction. **Predict and Set Purpose**

Ring! Ring! Ring!

It is the fire alarm! Anthony slides down the pole.

THUD!

He lands hard. But the thick rubber pad on the ground cushions his feet.

Let's **Think** About...

How do firefighters react to the alarm?

🔵 **Important Ideas**

Liz jumps into her boots and pulls up her fireproof pants. She checks the computer. It shows the fire is at 7 Oak Lane. In the truck Liz grabs the walkie-talkie. "Chief Miller! We're on our way!"

"Right!" says the fire chief.

He has gone ahead in a special fast car. "I'll meet you there."

Liz starts the engine as the firefighters jump in. She flips on the sirens and lights and drives out of the fire house. The truck speeds toward the fire.

Cars and buses stop and wait when they hear the siren coming.

The fire chief calls Liz. "I'm at the fire scene. It's an old house that's been empty for years. But someone saw a young boy playing on the porch this morning. He might be inside the house. Tell Dan and Anthony to get their air tanks ready."

"Okay, Chief," says Liz. "I can see the smoke from here. We'll be there in two minutes."

Let's Think About...

Besides the fire, what is the other problem in the story?

◎ Important Ideas

Liz turns the corner into Oak Lane. Flames cover the top of the house.

The fire is spreading quickly. There's no time to lose! Liz hooks a hose from the truck to the nearest fire hydrant. A pump on the truck pulls water from the hydrant to another hose. Liz and another firefighter point the hose at the flames. "Ready!" calls Liz.

WHOOSH!

They hold on tight as the water shoots out. It comes out of a fire hose hard enough to knock a person down.

Let's Think About...

What does this picture show about how fires burn?

🎯 Important Ideas

205

Let's Think About...

Three firefighters are holding the hose. What does this tell you about the hose?

○ Important Ideas

Anthony and Dan are ready to search the burning building. They have put on their air tanks and face masks. Each tank holds 40 minutes of air. That's not much time!

"The boy's name is Luke," the chief tells them.

"Right," says Anthony. He grabs a hose.

"Let's put the wet stuff on the red stuff!" says Dan.

Dan and Anthony run to the back of the house. The fire is not as bad here. Dan feels the back door. If it is hot, flames could leap out. "It's cold," says Dan. They step inside.

Thick black smoke is everywhere. Anthony shines his flashlight around. "Luke! Luke!" he calls. No one answers.

"I can hear fire upstairs," says Dan.

The fire has damaged the staircase. It could fall down at any time. They climb up the steps very slowly.

Outside, the outriggers are set down on the ground. Outriggers are like legs. They keep the truck steady as the ladder is raised. The ladder goes up like a telescope

Let's Think About...

Here's a good place to ask a question, such as "Why do firefighters touch the door?"
Questioning

207

to the top of the house. A hose runs up the side. The firefighter on the ladder shoots water down on the fire. The flames crackle and hiss. They get smaller, then suddenly jump even higher.

Inside the house, the fire rages. It is hot enough to melt glass. Anthony sprays water on the flames. Fire has made the house weak.

"It could come down any second," says Dan. "We must find Luke."

BOOM! A beam crashes down near them. But their helmets protect their heads. CRASH!

"Quick!" says Anthony. "We're running out of time."

They come to another door. But it will not open. Dan swings his ax at the door. Once. Twice. Three times. "It's jammed!" shouts Dan. The roar of the fire is so loud they can hardly hear. "We'll have to use the electric saw."

Let's Think About...

What does this photo tell you about firefighting?
Inferring

209

Anthony switches on the saw. WHRRR! He cuts a hole in the door big enough to climb through.

"Luke!" calls Dan. "Luke?" But the room is empty.

Suddenly the chief calls. "Get out now! The roof is coming down!"

Dan and Anthony race downstairs. They get out just as the roof falls in. "We didn't find Luke!" yells Dan.

"He's okay," says the chief. "We just found him up the block."

"Whew!" says Dan. "Good news!"

Hours later the flames are out. Anthony sprays water on the parts still glowing red. He is tired and dirty—and very hungry!

Liz winds the hoses back on to the truck. Finally she rests. She is tired too. Back at the station Anthony sits down to eat. "At last!" he says.

Suddenly a loud noise makes him jump. "Dinner will have to wait!" laughs Dan.

Ring! Ring! Ring!

Practice E.D.I.T.H.—Exit Drills in the Home

Do you know what to do if a fire starts in your home? Don't wait until it happens:

- Sit down with your family now.

- Talk about how you would get out of the house.

- Plan at least two ways out of every room.

- Decide where you will all meet once you get outside.

A fire drill now could save lives later!

Let's Think About...

Why does the author tell you to practice E.D.I.T.H.?

◉ Important Ideas

211

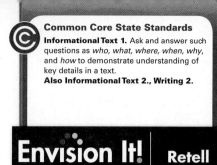

Common Core State Standards

Informational Text 1. Ask and answer such questions as *who, what, where, when, why,* and *how* to demonstrate understanding of key details in a text.
Also Informational Text 2., Writing 2.

Envision It! | Retell

READING STREET ONLINE
STORY SORT
www.ReadingStreet.com

Think Critically

1. This story tells about a day of a firefighter. How do firefighters help people in the community? Text to World

2. Why does the author tell you about a real fire? Think Like an Author

3. Find a fact on page 208. How can you tell it is a fact? Fact and Opinion

4. What is the important idea on page 200? What details support the idea? Important Ideas

5. Look Back and Write
Look back at page 207. Are the firefighters careful as they search for Luke? How do you know this is not a fictional story? Provide evidence to support your answer.

Key Ideas and Details • Text Evidence

Angela Royston

Angela Royston has written books about animals, plants, ships, trains, trucks, cars, and science. Royston was born in England and studied many different things at school. "I feel able to tackle almost any subject," she says. "I most like to work on books that are fun." She likes to read all she can about something before she writes about it.

Read two more books by Angela Royston.

Life Cycle of a Kangaroo

Strange Plants

Use the Reading Log in the *Reader's and Writer's Notebook* to record your independent reading.

Common Core State Standards
Writing 3. Write narratives in which they recount a well-elaborated event or short sequence of events, include details to describe actions, thoughts, and feelings, use temporal words to signal event order, and provide a sense of closure. **Also Language 1.**

Let's Write It!

Key Features of Narrative Nonfiction

- tells a story about real people or events

- usually shows events in the order they happened

READING STREET ONLINE
GRAMMAR JAMMER
www.ReadingStreet.com

Narrative

Narrative Nonfiction

Narrative nonfiction tells about real people and about things that really happen. The student model on the next page is an example of narrative nonfiction.

Writing Prompt Think about other community workers. Now write a narrative telling how one of these workers performs a job.

Writer's Checklist

Remember, you should ...

☑ tell what a real worker does.

☑ include strong verbs and exact nouns.

☑ say and write pronouns correctly.

214

Mr. Cooper is a mail carrier. He works in our town. We sent a letter and package to Mrs. Gavin across the road.

Even when rain pours and the wind chills him, Mr. Cooper delivers the mail. That happened last week.

Mr. Cooper walked a lot and put the mail in the right mailboxes. Mrs. Gavin was happy to get the package.

The **pronoun he** refers to Mr. Cooper. **We** also is a pronoun.

Writing Trait Word choice includes strong verbs (*pours, chills*) and exact nouns (*mailboxes*).

Genre This **narrative nonfiction** tells about a real worker.

Conventions

Pronouns

Remember A pronoun is a word that takes the place of a noun or nouns. The words **I, you, he, she, it, we,** and **they** are pronouns.

Liz starts the engine. **She** flips on the sirens and lights.   215

Social Studies in Reading

Genre
Drama

- *Drama* is another word for *play*.
- A drama is a story that is acted out for others.
- A drama has characters who have their own speaking parts called dialogue.
- A drama has a setting and a plot.
- Read "Firefighting Teamwork." Look for elements that make this story a drama.

N° 3 FIRE

FIREFIGHTING TEAMWORK

a play by Connie Carpenter

CHARACTERS:

Firefighter Kelly (FF KELLY)

Firefighter Sanchez (FF SANCHEZ)

Firefighter Johnson (FF JOHNSON)

Chief

Three or Four City Council Members

Scene: A firehouse. *(One firefighter is sweeping. Another is washing dishes. Another is sleeping.)*

FF KELLY: *(sweeping)* Boy, is this fire station dirty!

FF SANCHEZ: *(washing dishes)* Yeah, we all have to clean up the mud and dirt we tracked in. That last fire was a mess!

FF KELLY: I think Johnson worked really hard. He had to roll up that hose almost all by himself. That was hard work! He's probably upstairs taking a nap. *(Telephone rings.)*

FF KELLY: *(stops sweeping)* I'll get that. *(picks up phone)* Firefighter Kelly here.

CHIEF: *(voice from off stage)* Firefighter Kelly, this is the Chief.

FF KELLY: Yes, Chief. What is it?

CHIEF: We're having an inspection by the city council today. Is everything in shape?

FF KELLY: It will be, Chief. With teamwork we should be able to get things in tip-top shape for the inspection.

Let's **Think** About...

Who are the speakers on this page? How do you know?
Drama

Let's **Think** About...

How is dialogue used so far?
Drama

Let's **Think** About...

What are the firefighters doing in this part of the play? Why?
Drama

CHIEF: Good! I'll bring the council right over.

FF SANCHEZ: What? Is it a fire? an accident?

FF KELLY: No! The Chief is bringing over the city council for an inspection.

FF SANCHEZ: Uh-oh! We'd better hurry!

FF KELLY: What about our beds?

FF SANCHEZ: Johnson is up there. Do you think he made them?

FF KELLY: We'd better get up there and check! *(Both firefighters run up the stairs. Firefighter Johnson is lying on a bed, snoring.)*

FF KELLY: *(looks at beds)* Just as I thought! Unmade!

FF SANCHEZ: Johnson, wake up!

FF JOHNSON: What? What is it? *(wakes up and rises)* What's happening?

FF SANCHEZ: *(begins making bed)* We have to hurry. The Chief is bringing the city council over for an inspection.

218

FF JOHNSON: Inspection! Oh, no! Let's get this place cleaned up. *(begins making bed)*

FF KELLY: I'll get the broom. This place needs sweeping. I'll use the pole. It's faster. *(Fire alarm rings.)*

FF JOHNSON: The alarm!

FF SANCHEZ: This cleaning will have to wait. *(Firefighters slide down pole and put on their gear. Firefighter Sanchez checks fire board for location of fire and turns off alarm.)*

FF SANCHEZ: There! I've turned off the alarm. The fire is at 422 East Jay Street. Let's go! *(Firefighters exit; fire truck siren slowly fades away.)* *(Chief and council members arrive.)*

CHIEF: *(looking around)* This place looks great! Kelly, Johnson, Sanchez? *(Chief looks at fire board to find out where the firefighters have gone. He turns to council members.)* It looks like they've gone to another fire. Well, that's our fire department. They're hard workers, both in the fire station and in the community.

Let's **Think** About...

Reading Across Texts What did you learn about firefighters' jobs from the selections? Which job do you think is most important?

Writing Across Texts Write a brief paragraph to explain your answer.

219

Common Core State Standards
Foundational Skills 3.d. Decode words
with common prefixes and suffixes.
Also Foundational Skills 4.b.,
Speaking/Listening 1.a.

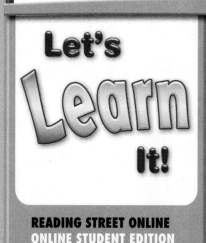

Let's Learn It!

READING STREET ONLINE
ONLINE STUDENT EDITION
www.ReadingStreet.com

Vocabulary

Suffixes

Word Structure A **suffix** is a word part that is added to the end of a word. A reader can use a suffix to help decide the meaning of a word.

safe   safely

The suffix **-ly** often means "in a certain way." **Safely** means "in a safe way."

Practice It! Add -ly to each word. Write the new word and its meaning.

shy   quiet   slow   sad

Fluency

Read with Accuracy

When you read, read the words you see. Blend the sounds to read the word. Check by putting the new word in the sentence to see if it makes sense.

Practice It! Take turns reading each sentence aloud to a partner.

1. The park is a great place to play baseball. Have you played there lately?

2. My cat, Patches, must be hungry. Look at Patches staring at the fish tank.

3. I was so tired that I quickly fell asleep while the movie played.

220

Media Literacy

Describe how media tells about culture.

Identify Cultural Characteristics in Media

The media is a source of information about culture, or the way people live. You can learn about your own and other cultures. You can see how your activities are alike and different. Maybe you play soccer. Lots of children around the world play soccer. That's one way you are all alike. You can use the media to find out other ways too.

Practice It! Work in groups. Find some articles about a holiday, such as Independence Day. Find out how people celebrate the holiday. Do you celebrate in the same way? What do you do that is different? Tell the class about the holiday and the ways people celebrate. When others are speaking, remember to listen attentively to them.

Tips

- Recognize informational purposes of media.
- When you speak to the class, use a louder voice than when you speak to a small group of friends.

Let's Talk About

Responsible Community Members

- Share information about community members solving problems.

- Share ideas about community members helping and respecting each other.

READING STREET ONLINE
CONCEPT TALK VIDEO
www.ReadingStreet.com

223

Common Core State Standards
Language 4.e. Use glossaries and beginning dictionaries, both print and digital, to determine or clarify the meaning of words and phrases. **Also Language 4.**

Envision It! | Words to Know

annoy

shrugs

signature

complain

mumbles

P.M.

READING STREET ONLINE
VOCABULARY ACTIVITIES
www.ReadingStreet.com

Vocabulary Strategy for

Dictionary Skills

Dictionary/Glossary While reading, you may come across a word you don't know. When you use a dictionary or glossary for help, you may find more than one definition, or meaning. Remember, a glossary is like a dictionary, but it is found in the back of some books. The words in a dictionary or glossary are listed in alphabetical order.

1. Use the guide words at the top of each page to find the entry for the word.

2. Read all the meanings given for the word.

3. Choose the meaning that makes the best sense in the sentence.

Read "Safety Solution." Use a dictionary or glossary to find the meanings of unknown words.

Words to Write Reread "Safety Solution." Write a letter asking the mayor to put a stop sign on Jamie's corner. Use words from the *Words to Know* list in your letter.

You've learned
1 6 9
Amazing Words
so far this year!

223

Common Core State Standards
Foundational Skills 3.d. Decode words with common prefixes and suffixes.

Envision It! | Sounds to Know

READING STREET ONLINE
SOUND-SPELLING CARDS
www.ReadingStreet.com

Phonics

Prefixes *un-, re-, pre-, dis-*

Words I Can Blend

unclear

renew

preheat

disagree

unbeaten

Sentences I Can Read

1. It was unclear whether we needed to renew our books.

2. Mom knew she must preheat the oven before baking.

3. Marcy and I disagree about which teams are unbeaten.

I Can Read!

My sister Abby is in preschool. When Abby first started, she disliked going. Now she is unhappy when it is time to go home. When Mom takes her to preschool, Abby disappears inside. Mom has her retrace her steps to kiss her good-bye. Last night Abby recited a story for us about a bunny that is untidy. It was a replay of part of a show the preschool put on. I was unprepared for how clever Abby is. I am so proud of her!

Common Core State Standards
Literature 1. Ask and answer such questions as *who, what, where, when, why,* and *how* to demonstrate understanding of key details in a text. **Also Literature 7.**

Envision It! | Skill Strategy

Skill

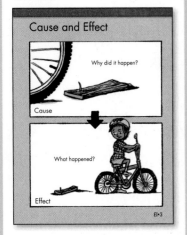

Strategy

READING STREET ONLINE
ENVISION IT! ANIMATIONS
www.ReadingStreet.com

Comprehension Skill

Cause and Effect

- As you read, look for what happened and why it happened.

- Clue words help you figure out what happened and why. *Because, so,* and *since* are clue words.

- Use what you learned about cause and effect to fill in a graphic organizer like this as you read "Put It on a Poster."

What happened	Why it happened

Comprehension Strategy

Visualize

As good readers read, they create pictures in their minds how something looks, sounds, feels, tastes, or smells. Creating sensory details can help you monitor and adjust your understanding of what you read. Visualizing makes reading more fun. When you read, create sensory details in your mind.

Put It on a Poster

Meg saw a problem on the playground at her school. No one was playing on the swing because the swing was broken. She told a teacher.

Jesse saw a problem too. He wanted people in his town to recycle instead of make trash. He wanted to tell many people at once, so he decided to make a poster. A poster is a big sign. It uses words and pictures to give a message.

Skill What caused Jesse to make the poster? What effect did the poster have?

To make a poster, you need large paper or board, markers or paint, and a pencil. First, decide on a message for your poster. Then, plan your poster with a pencil. That way you can erase if you make a mistake. Next, color or paint over the pencil marks. You can draw or cut out pictures to illustrate your poster. Finally, ask an adult before you hang up your poster.

Strategy Visualize the process of making a poster. Think about how the poster would look after each step.

Your Turn!

 Need a Review? See the *Envision It! Handbook* for additional help with cause and effect and visualizing.

▶ **Ready to Try It?** As you read *Carl the Complainer*, use what you've learned about cause and effect to understand the text.

227

Common Core State Standards

Language 4.e. Use glossaries and beginning dictionaries, both print and digital, to determine or clarify the meaning of words and phrases. **Also Language 4.**

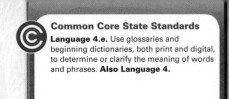

Envision It! Words to Know

annoy

shrugs

signature

complain

mumbles

P.M.

Vocabulary Strategy for

⊙ Dictionary Skills

Dictionary/Glossary While reading, you may come across a word you don't know. When you use a dictionary or glossary for help, you may find more than one definition, or meaning. Remember, a glossary is like a dictionary, but it is found in the back of some books. The words in a dictionary or glossary are listed in alphabetical order.

1. Use the guide words at the top of each page to find the entry for the word.

2. Read all the meanings given for the word.

3. Choose the meaning that makes the best sense in the sentence.

Read "Safety Solution." Use a dictionary or glossary to find the meanings of unknown words.

Words to Write Reread "Safety Solution." Write a letter asking the mayor to put a stop sign on Jamie's corner. Use words from the *Words to Know* list in your letter.

SAFETY SOLUTION

As Jamie and Anton come into the house, Jamie's mom is on the phone. She is saying, "It's just not safe!"

"What's up with your mom?" Anton mumbles. Jamie shrugs. Then Jamie's mom hangs up.

"What's wrong, Mom?" Jamie asks.

"Mrs. Johnson just called. Her little boy was almost hit by a car! On our street!"

"That's terrible," says Anton.

"Yes, cars drive too fast, at all hours. Even as late as 10:00 P.M.!" she says. "I wish there were something we could do besides complain."

Jamie has an idea. But he doesn't want to annoy his mother by talking too much. Finally, he speaks up.

"I have an idea," says Jamie. "We need a stop sign on our corner. Then cars can't race down the street."

"That's a great idea!" says Jamie's mom. "We'll write a petition for a stop sign. We'll ask Mrs. Johnson for her signature. We'll ask other neighbors too."

Jamie's mom gives Jamie a big hug and says, "This just might work!"

Your Turn!

❚❚ Need a Review? For more help with dictionary skills, see *Words!* on p. W·14.

▶ Ready to Try It? Read *Carl the Complainer* on pp. 230–247.

Genre

Realistic fiction tells about made-up events that could happen in real life. In this story you will read about a boy helping his community.

230

Carl the Complainer

Written by Michelle Knudsen
Illustrated by Maryann Cocca-Leffler

Question of the Week

How can we be responsible community members?

My friends say I complain a lot. They even call me Carl the Complainer.

But hey, some things are just so annoying!

Like TV jingles that get stuck in your head. And paper cuts.

It's five o'clock—the time the town park closes.

"Five P.M. is way too early for the park to close," I complain for about the millionth time.

We turn down Dale's street. "At least we've got a town park," he goes on. "Look —"

"I know, I know," I say, laughing. "Look on the bright side!"

Dale starts laughing.

"Keep it down out there!" Dale's next-door neighbor yells.

"Sorry, Mr. Henry," we both call out.

We go into Dale's house.

233

BUY SUPER CRUNCH CEREAL!

Sign our petition to save **POWER FRIENDS!**

CLICK HERE TO PLAY THE BEST GAME IN THE ENTIRE UNIVERSE!

Get your parents to buy you this! And this!

You could be a space monster on the next *ALIEN TURES!*

I show Dale a cool Web site. But an ad pops up—then four more. "Pop-up ads are so annoying," I complain. I start clicking them all closed.

"Wait!" says Dale. "There's a petition to save "Power Friends"! I want to sign it. I love that show."

"Why bother?" I say. "The best shows always get cancelled. It's so annoying."

"That's what the petition is about," Dale explains. "If the network sees that lots of kids like the show, they might keep it on."

"Can anyone start a petition?"

Dale shrugs. "Sure, I guess. Why?"

"Maybe *we* should start one," I say. "A petition to keep the park open later!"

"Great idea!" Dale says. "But how do we do it?"

"There's always the Internet," says Dale.

A few clicks later, we find a how-to site about petitions.

Perfect Petition Pointers

1. Give it a title (for example, "Petition to Make Bigfoot the New School Mascot").

2. Say whom it is addressed to.

3. Say who is sending it.

4. Say what you want to do or undo.

5. Get people to sign it—the more people, the better!

6. Give it to a person or group who has the power to do what you want to get done.

A petition is a written request. People sign a petition to show that they agree with the request. Many petitions are on the Internet, and some are passed around by hand.

Dale and I write up the petition and make copies. Then we get our friends together and tell them about our plan.

"I'll help collect signatures," says Laura.

"Me too!" adds Tony. "It would be great if the park stayed open later."

Mary and Pete want to help also!

Petition to Change Park Hours
To: Hanford Town Council
We, the following community members of Hanford, would like the town park to stay open later. We feel the kids of Hanford need a good place to play baseball (and other things). Grown-ups could stay in the park later too.

People have been writing petitions for thousands of years. Scientists have even found petitions in the tombs of ancient Egyptians.

We all take copies and split up into teams.

My parents are happy to sign. "That's two names already," I say. "This will be a snap!"

But Mrs. Monroe next door says, "Sorry, kids, now isn't a good time."

At the next house, Mr. Adams listens to about one sentence. "Not interested," he mumbles.

"Maybe we should try some place with more people," I suggest.

We try the train station.

We try the supermarket.

But most people are too busy to even listen to what we have to say.

We all meet up at Dale's. Everybody has been unlucky. "This is so annoying," I groan.

"There must be more people who want the park open later," says Laura.

"That's it!" I shout. "We should be talking to people at the park!"

"Yesssss!" everybody yells.

In the 1830s many Americans signed petitions to the U.S. government asking that slavery be stopped in the United States.

We sit around Dale's kitchen table and start brainstorming.

"I'll bring treats to give away," says Tony. "People will come for the treats, and then we'll tell them about the petition!"

"We'll need signs too," Mary chimes in.

We set up in the park early Saturday morning. The signs look great. Lots of people stop at the tables. They take treats. And most of them sign the petition!

By six o'clock we have ninety-nine signatures.

"If we could just get one more, we'd have an even hundred," I say. "Who haven't we asked?"

"There's always Mr. Henry," says Dale. "But—"

"Good thinking!" I tell him. "Let's go!"

"But—" Dale repeats.

I lead the way to Mr. Henry's house.

Dale gulps and presses the bell. Mr. Henry opens the door.

"Uh, hi," Dale starts. "We were wondering if maybe you would sign our petition to keep the park open later."

Every American has the right to petition the government. This right is guaranteed by the First Amendment to the Constitution!

"The park hours are just fine," Mr. Henry growls. He starts to close the door.

"Wait!" I call out.

"Mr. Henry, you're always complaining that we make too much noise. So maybe you should help us do something about it!"

"Oh, really? Like what?" he snaps.

"You could sign our petition!" I reply. "If the park's open later, we can stay there instead of playing in the street."

Just when I'm ready to give up, Mr. Henry smiles. "You actually have a point there, son," he says. "Tell you what. I'll sign your petition. I'll even get some folks in my writing group to sign it too."

"You're a writer?" I ask.

"Sure. That's why I need quiet."

We end up with 108 names. "I hope that's enough," I say. "The meeting is tomorrow!"

I'm very nervous on the night of the meeting.

Carl's petition is going to the town council, a part of the government. But lots of petitions go to businesses and organizations—from movie studios to sports teams to stores.

The council is sitting in the front of the room.

First, a lady stands up and tells them that dog licenses are too expensive.

Next, a man talks about putting a traffic light on Elm Street.

Then it's my turn.

"Good luck!" whispers Dale.

"My friends and I love the park," I say. "But it closes at five P.M. and that's *way* too early." I hold up

the petition. "All the people who signed this want the park to stay open later."

"I don't know," says the man with the moustache. "Is it a good idea to have kids playing in the park after five?"

"It's better than having them run around in the street," a lady in the audience replies.

That's when I notice Mr. Henry.

"We do play outside in the street when the park closes," I say. "Sometimes the noise bothers our neighbors."

I grin at Mr. Henry. "Keeping the park open later would solve that problem too."

Mr. Henry smiles. But the council members are still disagreeing.

What if they say no?

It's time for the vote. I hold my breath.

"All in favor of keeping the park open until sundown?" asks the lady with the glasses.

One by one, the council members raise their hands.

I can hardly believe it. Our petition worked!

Everybody claps and cheers.

Lots of real-life kids have started petitions. One second-grade class even wrote a petition that made the ladybug the official state insect of Massachusetts!

246

Dale gives me a high five.

"We did it!" he says. "And the best part is, now you'll have one less thing to complain about."

"Was my complaining really that bad?" I ask.

"Yup," Dale laughs. "It was—"

"I know," I say with a grin. "Really annoying!"

Common Core State Standards
Literature 3. Describe how characters
in a story respond to major events and
challenges. Also Literature 1., 7.,
Writing 2.

Envision It! | Retell

Think Critically

1. How was Carl a good community member? How can you be a good community member as Carl was?

Text to Self

2. Why do you think the author wrote about petitions? **Think Like an Author**

3. Why does Mr. Henry decide to sign the petition on page 242?

Cause and Effect

4. What do you see when you read about the park where Carl and his friends play? **Visualize**

5. Look Back and Write
Look back at page 236. What does the petition ask for? Use evidence to support your answer.

Key Ideas and Details • Text Evidence

Meet the Author and the Illustrator

MICHELLE KNUDSEN

Michelle Knudsen says, "I'm a writer, editor, book lover, movie lover, science fiction and fantasy addict, occasional community theater actress, allergy-sufferer, and cat lover, among other things." Ms. Knudsen lives in Brooklyn, New York, with her cat, Cleo.

MARYANN COCCA-LEFFLER

Maryann Cocca-Leffler has always been drawing and painting. When she was in high school, she painted a mural on the family's garage door! Her first studio was a corner of a basement, but now she lives in New Hampshire where she has a big studio full of light.

Read two more books by Michelle Knudsen.

Library Lion

A Moldy Mystery

Use the *Reader's and Writer's Notebook* to record your independent reading.

Common Core State Standards

Writing 3. Write narratives in which they recount a well-elaborated event or short sequence of events, include details to describe actions, thoughts, and feelings, use temporal words to signal event order, and provide a sense of closure. **Also Language 1.**

Narrative

Realistic Fiction

Realistic fiction is a made-up story about events that could happen in real life. The student model on the next page is an example of realistic fiction.

Writing Prompt Think about your community. Write a story about what Carl the Complainer might do to try to improve your community.

Let's Write It!

Key Features of Realistic Fiction

- characters and the setting seem real
- characters do things that could really happen
- story tells events one after another

Writer's Checklist

Remember, you should . . .

☑ tell about events that could really happen.

☑ say and use time-order words such as **first, next,** and **last.**

☑ say and write pronouns correctly.

Helping the Library

The library needed more books. Carl wanted to get more books for the library. First, he put up signs.

The signs asked people to give books to the library. Next, Carl got people to help the library. They sorted the books. The library thanked the helpers. Last, the library thanked Carl.

Writing Trait Organization
Writer uses words such as *first* and *next* to tell events in order.

The **pronoun he** takes the place of *Carl*. **They** is a plural pronoun.

Genre Realistic fiction tells about actions that real people could do.

Conventions

Singular and Plural Pronouns

Remember **I, he, she,** and **it** are pronouns that name one person or thing. **We** and **they** are pronouns that name more than one. **You** can mean one person or more than one.

251

Common Core State Standards
Literature 4. Describe how words and phrases (e.g., regular beats, alliteration, rhymes, repeated lines) supply rhythm and meaning in a story, poem, or song.

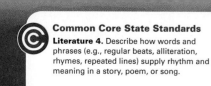

Social Studies in Reading

Genre
Poetry

- Poetry often has rhythm, rhyme, and repetition.

- Free verse is a form of poetry that may not have rhyme or a regular rhythm.

- Poetry helps you think about how things look, act, and sound.

- Read "Fishermen" and listen for its rhythm.

- Poetry often uses words that have different meanings from their ordinary meanings. Find the phrase "When night falls." Is this the literal, or real, meaning of the words? Or do these words mean something different?

"Fishermen"

by Juan Bautista Grosso
illustrated by Claudia Legnazzi

At dawn,

the fishermen

put out to sea

in their little boats.

They take their nets

and their songs,

these brave men of the sea.

When night falls,

they return to the harbor

loaded down

with the day's catch.

Black corvina,
pike and sole,
oysters and hake,
and much, much more.

When night falls
and kisses the homes
of the simple
sea folks,
the breeze sings
their boats to sleep
with a lullaby
of the sea.

CINA DEL PLATA

Let's Think About...

When you read the lines "the breeze sings/their boats to sleep/ with a lullaby/of the sea" what do you see in your mind's eye?

Let's Think About...

Reading Across Texts Carl the Complainer and "Fishermen" tell about different places and how they are used. How are the park and the sea used? Who or what belongs in each place? What happens in each place? Make a chart to answer these questions.

Writing Across Texts Write a short paragraph telling how the park and the sea are alike and different.

Common Core State Standards
Foundational Skills 4.b. Read on-level text orally with accuracy, appropriate rate, and expression on successive readings. **Also Speaking/Listening 6., Language 4.e.**

Let's **Learn** It!

READING STREET ONLINE
ONLINE STUDENT EDITION
www.ReadingStreet.com

Vocabulary

Dictionary Skills

Dictionary/Glossary A dictionary and a glossary give the definitions, or meanings, of words. Some words have more than one definition. These are multiple-meaning words. A dictionary will give the different meanings.

A dictionary shows different definitions for the word **wave.**

Practice It! Find these words in a dictionary or glossary. Write two different definitions for each word.

change   fair   tie   watch

Organize and Give a Demonstration

When you give a demonstration, you show others how to do something. During the demonstration, tell about each step as you show it. When seeing a demonstration, watch and listen carefully so you can restate and follow the instructions.

Practice It! Think about what you can demonstrate. You might show how to draw a flower or write a letter of the alphabet. Give oral instructions for each step in order. Then have a listener retell each step as he or she performs the activity.

Fluency

Accuracy and Appropriate Rate

Read at a pace so you understand the text. Blend the sounds to read new words. Check the new words in the sentence to be sure they make sense.

Practice It! Take turns reading the text below to a partner.

Carl and his parents went to an amusement park. Carl rode the bumper cars and merry-go-round. Carl's dad asked, "Do you want to ride the roller coaster?" Carl said, "I don't think so. It makes too many turns and goes too fast."

Common Core State Standards

Language 6. Use words and phrases acquired through conversations, reading and being read to, and responding to texts, including using adjectives and adverbs to describe (e.g., *When other kids are happy that makes me happy*). **Also Speaking/Listening 1.**

Let's Talk About

Responsible Animal Owners

- Share information about providing care for animals.

- Share ideas about training an animal.

READING STREET ONLINE
CONCEPT TALK VIDEO
www.ReadingStreet.com

256

You've learned

1 7 7

Amazing Words

so far this year!

257

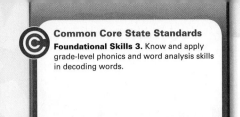
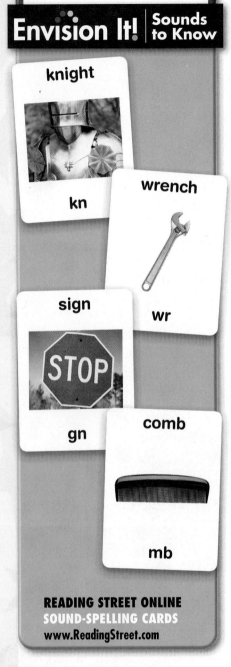

Phonics

Consonant Patterns
kn, wr, gn, mb

Words I Can Blend

knocking

wrist

gnat

know

li**mb**

Sentences I Can Read

1. Tim was knocking at our back door.

2. This tiny gnat landed on my wrist.

3. Did she know the girl sitting on that tree limb?

I Can Read!

I like to write, and I think I am pretty good at writing. Sometimes our teacher has us read our writing for our class. That scares me. My knees start to knock, my limbs tremble, and I gnash my teeth. Why does reading my writing make me go numb? Why does it tie me in knots? When I read my writing, it does not sound dumb. Do kids think I have a knack for writing? The kids are smiling! They must like it!

You've learned

🎯 Consonant Patterns *kn, wr, gn, mb*

Common Core State Standards

Foundational Skills 4.a. Read on-level text with purpose and understanding. **Also Literature 1.**

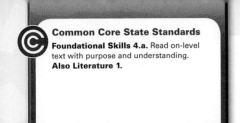

Envision It! | Skill Strategy

Skill

Strategy

READING STREET ONLINE
ENVISION IT! ANIMATIONS
www.ReadingStreet.com

Comprehension Skill

Plot and Theme

- The plot is what happens at the beginning, middle, and end of a story.

- Sometimes a story's theme, or "the big idea," is a lesson the author wants the reader to learn from the story.

- Use what you learned about plot and theme and use an organizer like this as you read "Trouble at the Table."

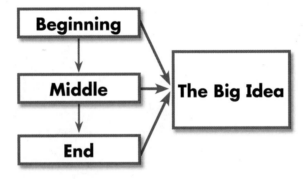

Comprehension Strategy

Background Knowledge

Good readers use background knowledge to help understand what they read. When reading, think about what you already know to help you monitor and adjust your understanding.

Trouble at the Table

Victor put his baby sister Sara in her highchair in the kitchen. He poured cereal into a bowl and filled a cup with milk. He placed them on the highchair tray.

"Enjoy."

Suddenly, she pounded her hands on her tray. Her cup tipped over, spilling the milk. Cereal flew onto the floor. She laughed the whole time.

Strategy Have you ever helped at home? How do you think helping makes Victor feel?

Victor sprang into action. He grabbed the cup and bowl. "What was I thinking?" he muttered.

He quickly found a cup with a lid and filled it with milk. He also grabbed a handful of paper towels. By the time his mom came downstairs, the mess was gone. Victor was feeding Sara. She was taking cereal from a spoon as Victor made airplane noises. He knew he solved the problem by staying calm.

Skill What happens at the end of the story? What lesson does Victor learn?

Your Turn!

 Need a Review? See the *Envision It! Handbook* for additional help with plot and theme and background knowledge.

▷ **Ready to Try It?** As you read *Bad Dog, Dodger!*, use what you've learned to understand the text.

Common Core State Standards
Language 4.e. Use glossaries and beginning dictionaries, both print and digital, to determine or clarify the meaning of words and phrases. **Also Language 5.**

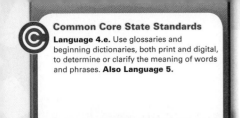

chased

practice

treat

chewing

dripping

grabbed

wagged

READING STREET ONLINE
VOCABULARY ACTIVITIES
www.ReadingStreet.com

Vocabulary Strategy for

Classify/Categorize

Dictionary/Glossary When you classify, or group, related words, you can understand their meanings. Think about how words are alike, or what they have in common. For example, *red*, *blue*, and *green* are all color words. You can classify them together. You can use a dictionary or a glossary to check if a word fits into a category.

1. Think of the category that a word might fit in.

2. Look for other words that fit in that category.

3. Use a dictionary or a glossary to check if a word fits in.

As you read "Rabbit Tricks," look for words that tell what the rabbit can do. Use a dictionary to check the meanings of words.

Words to Write Reread "Rabbit Tricks." If it were up to you, what would you train Homer to do? Write about it. Use words from the *Words to Know* list.

262

Rabbit Tricks

"You can't teach a rabbit to do tricks," said Eric.

"Why not?" asked Lucy. "Rabbits are smart. I can train Homer. Each time he does what I want, I'll give him a treat."

Eric looked at Homer, who was chewing on a lettuce leaf. He tossed a ball across the room. "Fetch, Homer," he said. Homer stayed perfectly still, the lettuce leaf dripping out of his mouth.

Lucy sighed. "Homer won't do dog tricks. He will learn to do rabbit tricks. It will just take some practice."

A week later, Lucy said to Eric, "Come and see what Homer can do." Lucy held a lettuce leaf in front of Homer and asked, "Homer, do you want this lettuce leaf?" She moved the leaf up and down. Homer's ears pricked up. Then he wagged his head up and down. "See? Homer answered me."

Eric grabbed the lettuce leaf and walked out of the room. Homer chased after him.

"See? Now he's playing Follow the Leader," said Lucy. "You *can* teach a rabbit to do tricks!"

Your Turn!

⏸ **Need a Review?** For more help with using a dictionary or glossary to classify and categorize words, see *Words!* on p. W·14.

▶ **Ready to Try It?** Read *Bad Dog, Dodger!* on pp. 264–277.

Bad Dog, Dodger!

by Barbara Abercrombie • illustrated by Laura Ovresat

Genre

Realistic fiction tells about made-up events that could happen in real life. Look for things that could really happen to a boy and his dog.

Sam wanted a dog.

"If you're a good boy," said his father.

"When you can take care of it yourself," said his mother.

Sam cleaned up his room. He ate carrots and broccoli. He stopped making monster noises at night to scare Molly, his older sister. He hung up his cap after baseball practice.

On the morning of his ninth birthday, Sam found a large box waiting for him. Inside was a puppy. He was black and soft and had big feet. Sam named him Dodger.

The whole family loved Dodger. Dodger licked their faces and curled up on their laps. He nibbled their shoelaces.

267

One day Dodger knocked the trash
all over the kitchen floor.

"Bad dog, Dodger!" said Sam.

Dodger wagged his tail and wanted
to play, but Sam was already late for
baseball practice.

When Molly was taking a bath one night, Dodger jumped into the tub with her. She started to scream. Dodger jumped out and raced through the house dripping water.

Sam and his father chased him with towels.

"Bad dog, Dodger!" yelled Sam.

"He's not bad," said his father. "He just wants to play."

One morning Sam found Dodger chewing his baseball cap. There was a big hole in it. Sam was so mad he almost cried.

They were eating dinner when Dodger pulled down the living room curtains. He wore them into the kitchen. He looked like a bride.

"I've had it," said Sam's mother. "This dog has to live outside."

The next day Dodger jumped over the fence and followed Sam to school and into his classroom.

He knocked over the hamster cage. He ate the cover off a spelling book. Sam's mother had to leave work to take Dodger home.

Saturday was Sam's first Little League game. He was up at bat when Dodger came flying onto the field.

The umpire yelled, "Time out!"

The other team booed.

The coach yelled, "Get that dog!"

271

Dodger grabbed the bat and ran around the field with it. The umpire and the coach ran after him. Sam had to leave the game to take Dodger home.

"We can't go on like this," said Sam's mother. "Maybe Dodger would be better off with somebody who had more time."

Sam knew his mother was right. Dodger needed more attention.

Sam went out and sat in the doghouse with Dodger. "I love you, Dodger." Dodger's tail thumped up and down. "But you need to practice being a good dog."

Suddenly Sam had an idea.

That night he set his alarm to go off half an hour early.

The family was still asleep when Sam got up
the next morning. In the kitchen he filled his pockets
with dog treats.

"Wake up, Dodger!"

Sam pitched a ball to Dodger. Dodger caught it.
"Good dog, Dodger!"

Sam waved a treat in the air. "Come!"

Dodger pranced around the yard with the ball
in his mouth. "This is training, not a game!" yelled Sam.

Finally Dodger set the ball down at Sam's feet. Sam
gave him a treat and said, "Good dog, Dodger!"

"Dodger's in spring training," Sam told his parents at breakfast.

Sam pitched balls to Dodger every morning. "Come, Dodger!" he'd shout, waving a treat when Dodger caught the ball.

"Sit!" And Sam would push Dodger's bottom down to show him what sit meant. "Stay!"

After a month of training, Sam decided Dodger was ready to come to a baseball game.

Dodger sat in the bleachers next to Sam's parents.

In the ninth inning, Sam was up at bat with two strikes and the bases loaded. The score was tied. The pitcher wound up to pitch. Everybody held their breath. Sam gripped the bat and hit a fly ball over the bleachers.

"Foul!" yelled the umpire.

Suddenly a flash of black fur leaped into the air to catch the ball.

Oh, no, thought Sam as the umpire called "Time out!" and the game stopped.

"That crazy dog again!" cried the coach. The other team was laughing. Sam's mother was shaking her head.

275

Dodger trotted toward Sam with the ball in his mouth. He dropped it at Sam's feet.

"Good dog," said Sam.

He walked Dodger to the dugout. "Sit." Dodger sat.

All the spectators grew very quiet. The other team stopped laughing.

"Stay," said Sam.

Dodger stayed.

Sam hit the next pitch right over the fence for a home run. He ran to first, second, third base.

As he reached home plate, he called, "Come, Dodger!" and everyone clapped. Even the coach.

After the game, the team had their
picture taken. Dodger was in the front row
and got to wear Sam's baseball cap.

Common Core State Standards

Literature 7. Use information gained from the illustrations and words in a print or digital text to demonstrate understanding of its characters, setting, or plot. **Also Writing 3.**

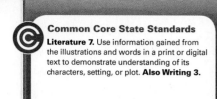

Think Critically

1. Sam got a puppy for his birthday. Do you know someone who has a pet? How is having a pet work, and how is it fun? Text to Self

2. According to the author, what skills does a good pet owner have?

Think Like an Author

3. What did Sam learn about owning a pet? Plot and Theme

4. What do you know or what have you read about training a pet? How did that help you understand Sam and Dodger? Background Knowledge

5. Look Back and Write Look back at pages 273–274. What does Sam compare Dodger's training to? Provide evidence to support your answer.

Key Ideas and Details • Text Evidence

Meet the Author

Barbara Abercrombie

Barbara Abercrombie began writing stories when she was six years old. She likes to write about pets. "When my children were growing up, we had dogs. Our favorite was a Newfoundland named Jennifer. She looked like a large black bear and was often naughty, but we loved her very much. We let her sleep in our beds with the cats." Ms. Abercrombie has two cats now, Stuart Little and Charlotte Webb. Two of her books are about cats.

Read two more books by Barbara Abercrombie.

Charlie Anderson

Michael and the Cats

Use the *Reader's and Writer's Notebook* to record your independent reading.

Reading Log

279

Common Core State Standards
Writing 3. Write narratives in which they recount a well-elaborated event or short sequence of events, include details to describe actions, thoughts, and feelings, use temporal words to signal event order, and provide a sense of closure. **Also Language 1.**

Let's Write It!

Key Features of a Journal Entry

- tells about a personal event or idea
- tells what the writer thinks or feels
- may include the date

READING STREET ONLINE
GRAMMAR JAMMER
www.ReadingStreet.com

Narrative

Journal Entry

A **journal** is a person's book to write day-by-day entries about events in his or her life. The student model on the next page is an example of a journal entry.

Writing Prompt Think about the fun Sam has with his dog. Now write a journal entry that Sam might write telling about a new adventure with Dodger.

Writer's Checklist

Remember, you should . . .

☑ write as you think Sam would write in his journal.

☑ tell about an adventure with Dodger.

☑ say and use the pronouns I and **me** correctly.

June 9

Today Dodger showed he is a good swimmer. I took him to the beach with me. I threw a stick. It went into the lake. Before I knew it, Dodger swam out to get it. Then he brought it back to me. I can't wait to take Dodger to the beach again!

Pronouns
I and *me* take the place of Sam's name.

Genre
A **journal entry** often describes an event of one day.

Writing Trait Voice
The writer made it seem like Sam wrote the entry.

Conventions

Using I and Me

Remember Use **I** as a subject of a sentence. Use **me** after action verbs or after words such as *with* and *to*. Write *I*, not *i*. If you mention yourself and another person, name yourself last. Al and **I** read a story. It made Al and **me** laugh.

281

Common Core State Standards
Informational Text 6. Identify the main purpose of a text, including what the author wants to answer, explain, or describe. **Also Informational Text 7.**

Genre
Procedural Text

- Procedural text tells how to do something.

- Procedural text gives directions, or steps, to follow.

- Procedural text has captions and illustrations that help a reader understand what to do.

- Read "How to Train Your Puppy." Watch for numbered steps that help you follow this procedural text.

How to Train Your Puppy

by L. B. Coombs

Have you ever tried to make a puppy behave? Training a puppy means making it do the same thing over and over again. You can train a puppy or almost any pet. Here's how.

- Begin training when your puppy is very young.

- Teach your puppy to do only one new thing at a time.

- Pick one word as the command for each new thing you want the puppy to learn, but don't repeat the command too many times.

The words and pictures that follow will help you train your puppy.

1

First, let your puppy get to know you. Let him sniff your hand. He will learn to know you by your smell.

2

When you want your puppy to bark, say "Speak." Don't say "Talk" one day and "Bark" the next. Use the same word every time.

Speak!

Let's Think About...

This article uses numbers to list directions. Teaching a puppy to bark is which step?
Procedural Text

3 Do not yell at your puppy. This might scare him. Say "No" firmly and in a deep voice. If "No" is the word you want him to remember, use it all the time. Do not say "Stop" or "Don't" when you mean "No."

No!

4 Train your puppy to walk on a leash. Hold your end of the leash loosely. Don't pull your puppy with the leash. Play with your puppy while he is on the leash. It will help him get used to it.

Let's **Think** About...

Look at this illustration. What does it show? How does it help you understand Step 5?
Procedural Text

5 After your puppy has done what you ask, tell him he did a good job. Reward him with a treat. Hug and pat your puppy. Training will be fun for both of you.

284

6

You might want to teach your puppy to sit and stay. When your puppy is standing, gently push his bottom to the ground and say "Sit." After your puppy sits, say "Stay." When your puppy sits and stays for a while, praise him and give him a treat.

Sit!

Stay!

It takes time to train a puppy. But if you choose to do it, this training time can be good for both of you. You and your puppy will build a special friendship.

Let's Think About...

Reading Across Texts In *Bad Dog, Dodger!*, which rules from "How to Train Your Puppy" did Sam use?

Writing Across Texts Choose another rule and write a note to Sam explaining why he should follow this rule with Dodger.

Common Core State Standards
Foundational Skills 4.a. Read on-level text with purpose and understanding. **Also Speaking/Listening 1., Language 4.e.**

READING STREET ONLINE
ONLINE STUDENT EDITION
www.ReadingStreet.com

Vocabulary

Classify/Categorize

Dictionary/Glossary When you **classify** words, you put the words in **categories.** You can use a dictionary or glossary to help you decide if a word belongs in a category. You can classify *apple*, *banana*, and *grapes* as names of fruit.

Practice It! Classify these words into two categories. Tell what the words have in common.

blue	**boots**	**coat**
green	**hat**	**yellow**

Fluency

Expression and Intonation

Punctuation marks show how you should read text. Let your voice go up at the end of a question. Use your voice to show strong feeling when you see an exclamation mark.

Practice It! Read each sentence with expression and tone.

1. Everyone jumped out and yelled "Surprise!"

2. Hey! Let's go to the park and play ball!

3. Do you think we will win the game? I hope so!

Listening and Speaking

Listen carefully for facts and opinions when others speak.

Listen for Facts and Opinions

A statement of fact can be proven true or false. A statement of opinion tells someone's ideas or feelings. When listening to others, listen carefully for facts and opinions. The clue words **I think, should,** and **best** often show opinions.

Practice It! Read the sentences with a partner. Identify one fact and one opinion. Tell how you can prove the facts. Then, write down a new list of facts and opinions with your partner.

Bad Dog, Dodger! is the best story ever. It is about a dog named Dodger. He has four legs and a tail. I think everyone should read this story.

Tips

- Listen for clue words to identify facts and opinions.
- Make appropriate contributions to the class discussion.

287

Oral Vocabulary

Let's Talk About

Responsible Friends and Neighbors

- Share information about friends and neighbors communicating with one another.

- Share ideas about friends and neighbors respecting each other.

READING STREET ONLINE
CONCEPT TALK VIDEO
www.ReadingStreet.com

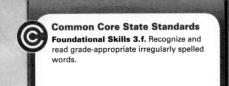

Envision It! Sounds to Know

phone — ph
laugh — gh
lock — ck
swing — ng

READING STREET ONLINE
SOUND-SPELLING CARDS
www.ReadingStreet.com

Phonics

Consonant Patterns *ph, gh, ck, ng*

Words I Can Blend

p h o n e

l a u g h i n g

s t a c k

t h i n g

t r u c k

Sentences I Can Read

1. Amy was laughing on the phone with her mom.

2. Can you see over that stack of books?

3. What is this red thing in the truck?

290

I Can Read!

Zack likes to sing funny songs. His pals pick songs that make him laugh. They phone him with laughter in their voices. They bring him stacks of songs with funny phrases.

Mom asks, "Is this a phase? Zack has a nice voice. Pretty songs are not tough to sing. Are funny songs the only thing Zack will sing?"

Zack says, "No, Mom. All kinds of songs bring me joy!" Mom now has a photograph of Zack singing pretty songs.

You've learned

◉ Consonant Patterns *ph*, *gh*, *ck*, *ng*

291

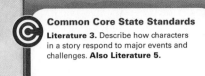

Skill

Strategy

Comprehension Skill

Character and Setting

- Characters are people or animals in a story.

- Setting is when and where a story takes place.

- As you read "Best Friends," use what you learned about character and setting to describe them in a chart like the one below.

What the Characters Do	What the Characters Say	Where the Story Takes Place

Comprehension Strategy

Story Structure

Good readers think about the order of events of a story. This can help you remember what you read. Then you can retell what happens. As you read "Best Friends," think about the important events of the story. Then retell the story in the right order to a partner.

Best Friends

Tara and Crystal were friends. One day, Tara said, "Let's draw all the things we will do next week."

Skill Who are the characters in the story?

The girls drew chalk pictures on the sidewalk. The girls drew pictures of the pool and a jump rope. They had fun together.

The next morning, Crystal fell and broke her arm. She went to the doctor. The doctor put her arm in a cast.

The next week, Tara went swimming by herself. She jumped rope too. She sighed and frowned. *Nothing is fun. I miss Crystal*, she thought.

Strategy Retell what has happened so far in the story. What happened first?

So Tara went to see Crystal. Crystal frowned. "I can't swim," she said. "I can't jump rope either." So the two girls played games. They made a tent with a blanket. They talked and laughed. They did not go swimming or jump rope, but they were happy together.

Skill What is the setting of the story here? Describe Crystal's feelings. How do you know?

Your Turn!

Need a Review? See the *Envision It! Handbook* for additional help with character and setting and story structure.

Ready to Try It? As you read the story, use what you've learned to understand the text.

293

Envision It! Words to Know

climbed

exploring

wondered

adventure

clubhouse

greatest

truest

READING STREET ONLINE
VOCABULARY ACTIVITIES
www.ReadingStreet.com

Vocabulary Strategy for

◎ Compound Words

Word Structure When you are reading, you may come across a long word that you don't know. If the long word is made up of two small words, then it is probably a compound word. The two small words can help you figure out the meaning of the compound word.

1. Look for the small words in the compound word.

2. Think of the meaning of each small word. Put the meanings together. Does this help you understand the meaning of the compound word?

3. Try the meaning in the sentence. Does it make sense?

Read "Boris and Cloris." Use the meanings of the small words to help you understand the meanings of the compound words.

Words to Write Reread "Boris and Cloris." Write about what you like to do with a friend. Use words from the *Words to Know* list.

Boris and Cloris

Boris, a mouse, lived on a farm. His home was in a haystack. He was bored. All he did was eat seeds. He longed for adventure.

At the far end of the cornfield was a small building. Boris wondered what was in it.

He asked his friend Cloris to go exploring with him, but she said no. She wanted to stay near the farmhouse. So Boris went alone.

When he got to the building, Boris climbed through a hole in a board. Two girls were sitting on the floor, talking.

"Who will we allow in our clubhouse?" asked one girl.

"Only the greatest and truest of our friends," said the other girl. "We will play baseball after school. But, look! There's a mouse in our clubhouse!"

The two girls tried to catch Boris. He raced for the hole, but where was it? "Over here, Boris," Cloris squeaked. Boris jumped through the hole, and they dashed across the cornfield.

When they were safe at the haystack, Boris said to Cloris, "Thank you for coming after me."

Your Turn!

⏸ **Need a Review?** For more help with using word structure to find the meaning of compound words, see *Words!* on p. W•9.

▷ **Ready to Try It?** Read *Horace and Morris but mostly Dolores* on pp. 296–313.

Horace and Morris

Genre

Fantasy is a make-believe story that could never happen in the real world. What makes this story a fantasy?

but mostly Dolores

by James Howe

illustrated by Amy Walrod

Question of the Week

How can we be responsible friends and neighbors?

Horace and Morris but mostly Dolores
loved adventure. They sailed the seven sewers.

They climbed Mount Ever-Rust. They dared to go where no mouse had gone before.

Horace and Morris but mostly Dolores never said,
"This is something we shouldn't do."

They said, "This is something we've *got* to do!"
And so there was almost nothing they didn't do.

Horace and Morris and Dolores were friends—the greatest of friends, the truest of friends, the now-and-forever-I'm-yours sort of friends. And then one day . . . Horace and Morris had a decision to make.

They didn't want to do anything without Dolores, but as Horace pointed out, "A boy mouse must do what a boy mouse must do."

"Bet you can't say *that* three times real fast," Dolores said with a smile.

302

Horace and Morris didn't even try. They didn't even smile.

"Good-bye, Dolores," they said.

What kind of place doesn't allow girls? Dolores wondered as she watched her friends step through the door of the Mega-Mice clubhouse.

Downhearted, Dolores went on her way—alone. It wasn't long before . . . Dolores had a decision to make.

She didn't really want to do anything without Horace and Morris, but she figured a girl mouse must do what a girl mouse must do. (She said this aloud three times real fast just to prove that she could.)

A GIRL MOUSE MUST DO WHAT A GIRL MOUSE MUST DO.

TODAY'S PROJECT:
GIFTS FOR
MOTHER
MADE FROM
Muenster

I'll bet Horace and Morris couldn't do that, she thought. But she wasn't smiling as she stepped through the door of the Cheese Puffs clubhouse.

Day after day, Dolores went to the Cheese Puffs. Day after day, Horace and Morris went to Mega-Mice.

They missed playing with each other, but as they said . . . "A girl mouse must do what a girl mouse must do." "A boy mouse must do what a boy mouse must do."

Horace and Morris and even Dolores were sure their friendship would never be the same. But then one day . . . Dolores made a different decision.

305

"I'm bored," she announced.

The other girls stared.

"Anybody here want to build a fort? How about a Roque-fort?"

The other girls booed.

"Okay, forget the cheese. I'm sick of making things out of cheese anyway. Let's go exploring."

The other girls gasped.

"Phooey!" said Dolores. "I quit!"

"If you quit, then I quit too!" a small voice said from the back of the room.

307

Outside Dolores introduced herself. "I'm Dolores."
"I'm Chloris," said the girl.

"Now where can we go to have some *real* fun around here?" Dolores thought and thought. "I've got it!" she said at last.

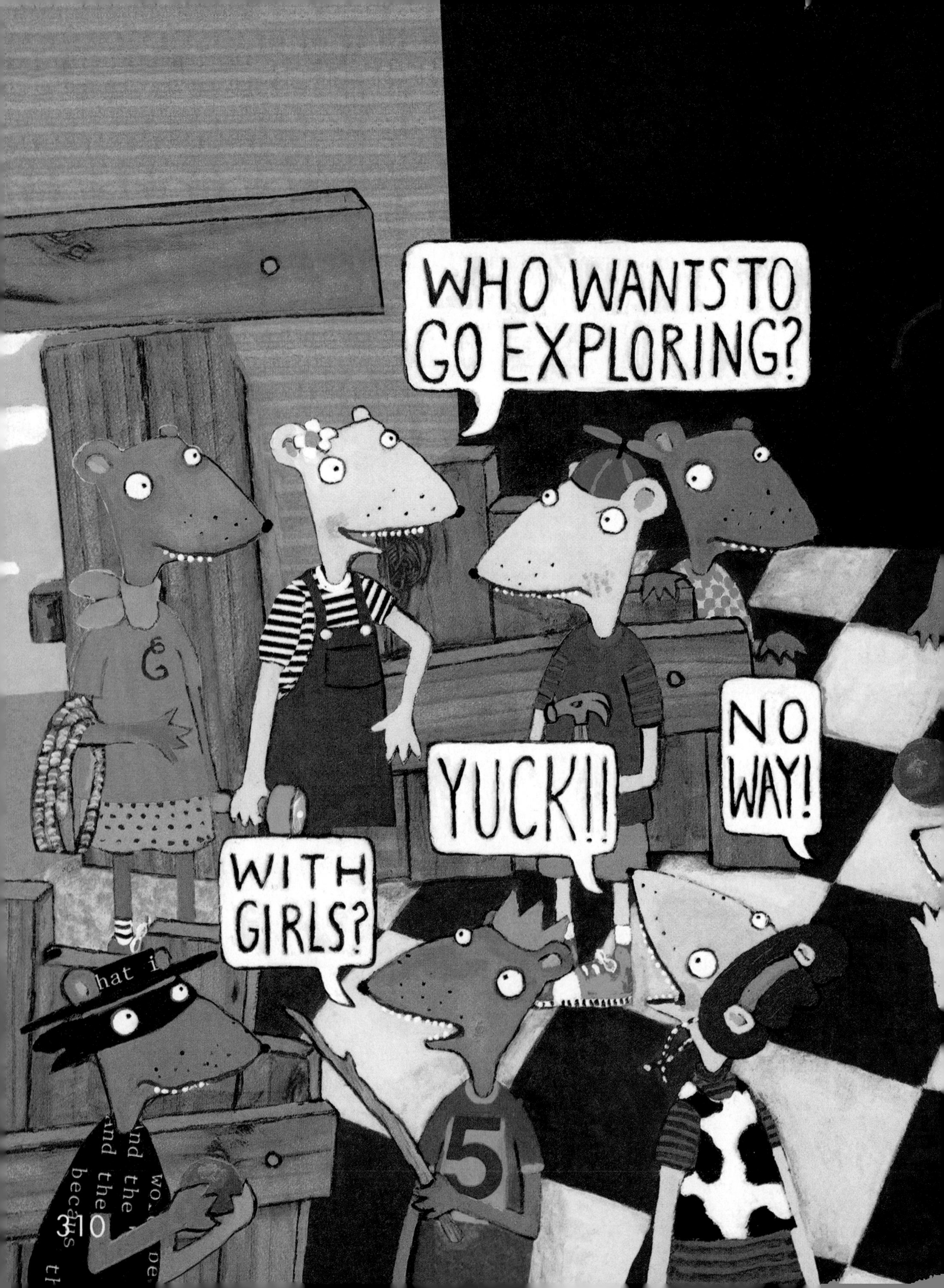
WHO WANTS TO GO EXPLORING?
WITH GIRLS?
YUCK!!
NO WAY!

311

The five friends spent the rest of the day
exploring, Chloris and Boris and Horace and
Morris . . . but mostly Dolores . . .

And the next day they built a clubhouse of their own.

Common Core State Standards
Literature 7. Use information gained from the illustrations and words in a print or digital text to demonstrate understanding of its characters, setting, or plot.
Also Literature 5., Writing 3.

Envision It! | Retell

READING STREET ONLINE
STORY SORT
www.ReadingStreet.com

Think Critically

1. Horace, Morris, and Dolores do a lot of things together. What do you and your friends like to do together?
Text to Self

2. What message do you think the author of this funny story is trying to give you? **Think Like an Author**

3. How did things change for each main character? Where did these changes happen? **Character and Setting**

4. What happens in the story to bring the friends back together?
Story Structure

5. Look Back and Write
Look back at page 306. Why does Dolores change her mind about the clubhouse? Provide evidence to support your answer.
Key Ideas and Details • Text Evidence

314

Meet the Author and the Illustrator

James Howe

James Howe began writing stories and plays when he was a boy. Mr. Howe has written more than 70 books about funny characters, including *Bunnicula* and *Pinky and Rex*. He thinks that the best way to be a good writer is to read and write, write, write!

Amy Walrod

Amy Walrod's first picture book was *Horace and Morris but mostly Dolores.* Ms. Walrod collects toys, lunch boxes, cupcake ornaments, sparkly things, and stuff she finds on the ground. Can you find any of the things she likes to collect in her pictures?

Read more books written by James Howe or illustrated by Amy Walrod.

Horace and Morris Join the Chorus (but what about Dolores?)

The Little Red Hen (Makes a Pizza)

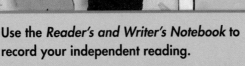

Use the *Reader's and Writer's Notebook* to record your independent reading.

Common Core State Standards
Writing 3. Write narratives in which they recount a well-elaborated event or short sequence of events, include details to describe actions, thoughts, and feelings, use temporal words to signal event order, and provide a sense of closure.
Also Language 1.

Narrative

Animal Fantasy

Animal fantasy stories tell about things that cannot happen in the real world. The characters are animals that act like people and usually talk. The student model on the next page is an example of an animal fantasy.

Writing Prompt Think about animal characters you would like to write about. Now write a fantasy about an adventure these friends have together.

Key Features of an Animal Fantasy

- characters are make-believe animals
- characters do things that real animals cannot do

READING STREET ONLINE
GRAMMAR JAMMER
www.ReadingStreet.com

Writer's Checklist

Remember, you should . . .

☑ tell about animals doing things that real animals cannot do.

☑ write a beginning, middle, and end in your story.

☑ say and use pronouns correctly.

Vera and Vic

Vera and Vic were bunnies. Vic asked Vera what they should do today.

"Let's sail across the sea," Vera said to him. They built a boat from a big plastic bottle.

They put it in a huge puddle. Then the boat carried them to a land far away.

Pronouns such as *they*, *him*, and *them* appear in different places in sentences.

Genre
In an **animal fantasy**, characters do things that real animals cannot do.

Writing Trait Conventions
The writer uses the correct pronouns as subjects and after action verbs.

Conventions

Different Kinds of Pronouns

Remember The pronouns **I, he, she, we,** and **they** are used as subjects of sentences. The pronouns **me, him, her, us,** and **them** are used after action verbs. The pronouns **you** and **it** can be used anywhere in a sentence.

317

Common Core State Standards
Informational Text 2. Identify the main topic of a multiparagraph text as well as the focus of specific paragraphs within the text. **Also Informational Text 5., 6.**

Social Studies in Reading

Genre
Magazine Article

- Magazine articles are examples of expository text.

- Magazine articles give information about a topic.

- Magazine articles tell about people, places, and activities.

- Magazine articles have graphics and captions that help tell about the topic.

- Read "Good Kicking." Look for how the writer gives information in the magazine article.

Good Kicking

by Rich Richardson
Staff Writer

From spring to fall, you can hear the whoops and hollers of happy children. What's happening? They are playing one of the fastest growing sports around—soccer!

Soccer is played in almost every country in the world. Boys and girls of all ages love this fast-moving sport. Soccer is played in schools and parks across America. Some towns have put together teams of children that play each other.

The small towns around Chicago have some of the best young soccer players. Some children begin playing on teams when they are as young as four or five.

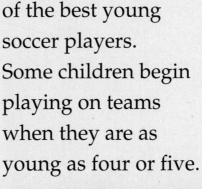

These players chase down the ball.

Good kicking means good footwork.

Let's **Think** About...

Look at the photos and captions. What is the topic of the article?
Magazine Article

Let's **Think** About...

In what countries do people play soccer? What does this tell you about soccer?
Magazine Article

319

"We want everyone to have fun," says Coach Kay of the Goalers, a team of seven-year-olds. "We have a mixed team of boys and girls. They learn to play together as they learn the rules of the game. Most importantly, they learn what it means to be a part of a team."

Anyone who has ever played a team sport knows that each team member is important. Team members have a responsibility to do the best job they can. If each team member does his or her job right, the team has fun and everybody wins.

"It's always nice to win," Coach Kay states.

Trident players chase down the ball for their team.

Two members of the Scooters congratulate each other.

Let's **Think** About...

Why did the writer write that team members "have a responsibility to do the best job they can"? **Magazine Article**

Coach Kay and members of the Goalers relax before a game. "Being part of a team is more than just winning," Coach Kay says.

"But it's also important that children have fun. Being part of a team is more than just winning. It's learning your role as a team member and knowing your responsibility to your fellow teammates. If we all work together, everybody wins."

Coach Kay should know. Her team, the Goalers, has not lost a game all season. The laughter and smiles on the children's faces also show that they have fun.

Let's **Think** About...

What is the main idea of the article? How can you distinguish it from the topic?
Magazine Article

Let's **Think** About...

Reading Across Texts Do you think Dolores would have liked playing soccer for the Goalers and Coach Kay?

Writing Across Texts Write a short paragraph telling why you feel as you do.

Common Core State Standards
Foundational Skills 4.b. Read on-level text orally with accuracy, appropriate rate, and expression on successive readings.
Also Speaking/Listening 4.

Let's

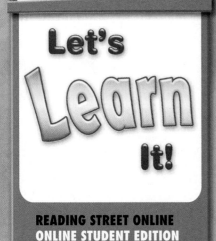

Learn
It!

READING STREET ONLINE
ONLINE STUDENT EDITION
www.ReadingStreet.com

Vocabulary

Compound Words

A compound word is a long word that is made up of two or more small words.

Starfish is a compound word made up of **star** and **fish**.

starfish

Practice It! Read the compound words. Identify the words that make up the compound word.

**doghouse   mailbox
outside   weekend**

Fluency

Read with Expression (Characterization)

When reading a story aloud, pay attention to quotation marks. Quotation marks let you know when someone is talking. Read the words inside the quotation marks as though you are the character speaking.

Practice It! Read aloud pages 306–309 of *Horace and Morris but mostly Dolores.* Read the words the characters say as though you are the characters.

322

Listening and Speaking

Maintain focus when presenting.

Maintain Focus in Narrative Presentation

When you tell a story, be sure to stay focused. Name the characters, describe the setting, and tell the events in the order they happen. Start with the beginning. Then tell what happens in the middle and the end. Speak clearly when telling the story so that listeners can follow what happens. Do not rush through the story. When listening to a story, listen to find out what happens to the characters.

Practice It! Think of a story you have read. Tell the story to the class. Remember to speak clearly. Maintain focus, and tell the story in order from beginning to middle to end.

Tips

- Describe the characters as you tell the story's sequence of events.

- Use conventions of language, including pronouns such as *he* and *him,* correctly.

Common Core State Standards

Language 6. Use words and phrases acquired through conversations, reading and being read to, and responding to texts, including using adjectives and adverbs to describe (e.g., *When other kids are happy that makes me happy*). **Also Speaking/Listening 1.**

Oral Vocabulary

Let's Talk About

Making Mistakes

- Share information about what happens if rules are broken.

- Share ideas about why rules have a purpose.

READING STREET ONLINE
CONCEPT TALK VIDEO
www.ReadingStreet.com

324

You've learned **193** Amazing Words so far this year!

325

Envision It! | Sounds to Know

hawk
aw

audience
au

daughter
augh

chalk
al

Phonics

◎ Vowel Patterns *aw, au, au(gh), al*

Words I Can Blend

s a u c e r

p a w

t a u g h t

p a u s e

c h a l k b o a r d

Sentences I Can Read

1. The saucer fell near the kitty's paw.

2. My coach taught me not to pause.

3. Let's show Dad on the chalkboard.

I Can Read!

When Paul was small, he crawled before he could walk. His mom always caught him before he could fall. His dad taught him to ride a trike before a bike. Paul would pause before beginning to talk. Now Paul is no longer small. He can walk and talk and ride a bike without help. He can draw and write and put together jigsaw puzzles. Paul is proud of all he can do.

You've learned

🔵 Vowel Patterns *aw, au, au(gh), al*

Common Core State Standards
Informational Text 2. Identify the main topic of a multiparagraph text as well as the focus of specific paragraphs within the text. **Also Informational Text 6.**

Envision It! | Skill Strategy

Skill

Main Idea and Details

Main Idea
What is the selection all about?

Details

EI•11

Strategy

Envision It! | Visual Strategies Handbook

Inferring

When we **infer** we use background knowledge with clues in the text to come up with our own ideas. We do this to support understanding.

PARK

CLOSED

Let's Think About Reading!

When I infer, I ask myself
• What do I already know?
• How does this help me understand what happened?

EI•20

**READING STREET ONLINE
ENVISION IT! ANIMATIONS**
www.ReadingStreet.com

Comprehension Skill

Main Idea and Details

- The main idea is the most important idea in a selection.

- A main idea is often stated in a sentence within the first or second paragraph.

- Use what you learned about identifying the main idea and follow the organizer below as you read "The BIGGEST Signs."

What the 1st paragraph tells you
What the 2nd paragraph tells you
What the 3rd paragraph tells you
What the 4th paragraph tells you

→ **What the story is all about**

Comprehension Strategy

Inferring

Good readers use what they know and what they read to make inferences. They make good guesses about the story. As you read "The BIGGEST Signs," think about why companies use billboards. How do you know? Write what you think and share it with a partner.

The BIGGEST Signs

You've probably seen them next to a road. Maybe you've seen one on top of a building. They are huge signs that tell you where to shop or what to eat. These have been around for a long time.

In the United States, the first billboards were made more than one hundred years ago. The first big signs were circus signs. They told people when the circus was coming. The signs had pictures of clowns and other acts.

Soon many companies were using billboards. They also started adding lights to billboards. Now people could see these big signs at night. Many billboards were put up next to highways, because people were driving more.

Today some billboards have parts that move. Some even have screens that show short movies. Think about billboards that you have seen.

Strategy Why do you think these signs are so big?

Skill What is the main idea of this paragraph?

Skill What is the topic of this selection? What is the main idea of the selection?

Your Turn!

Need a Review? See the *Envision It! Handbook* for additional help with main idea and inferring.

Ready to Try It? As you read the story, use what you've learned to understand the text.

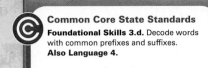

idea

signmaker

townspeople

afternoon

blame

important

Vocabulary Strategy for

🎯 Suffixes

Word Structure Suffixes are word parts added to the ends of words to change their meanings. You can use the meaning of a suffix to help you figure out the meaning of a word. The suffix *-less* usually means "without ____." For example, *careless* means "without care."

1. Put your finger over the *-less* suffix.

2. Look at the base word. Put the base word in the phrase "without ____."

3. Try that meaning in the sentence. Does it make sense?

Read "Sigmund's Sign." Look for words that end with *-less*. Use the suffix to help you figure out the meanings of the words.

Words to Write Reread "Sigmund's Sign." What sign do you think Sigmund will paint next? Write a paragraph about it. Use words from the *Words to Know* list.

Sigmund's Sign

Sigmund was a signmaker. He always had an endless list of jobs to do. Every shop, every building, and every house in the town had one of Sigmund's signs. The signs told what was sold in the shop (Toys) or who worked in the building (Police) or who lived in the house (The Guntersons). The signs helped the townspeople find their way around the town.

But Sigmund thought that signs could do much more than that. One cloudless afternoon, a large sign appeared in the town square. It said, "Don't blame them." People stopped to read it. Then they talked about the sign. They wondered what the sign meant. They thought about their own actions. Who was blameless? Had they been unfair?

Sitting in his signmaking shop, Sigmund smiled. He knew that a sign could do more than help people find their way around. A sign could make people think about an important idea. Sigmund began to paint another large sign.

Your Turn!

⏸ Need a Review? For more help with using suffixes to determine the meanings of words, see *Words!* on p. W·6.

▶ Ready to Try It? Read *The Signmaker's Assistant* on pp. 332–347.

SIGNMAKER'S ASSISTANT

Genre

Humorous fiction is a funny story about imaginary people and events. Look for the funny things that happen in this story.

THE SIGNMAKER's ASSISTANT

by Tedd Arnold

Question of the Week

How can we be responsible when we make a mistake?

Everyone in town agreed. The old signmaker did the
finest work for miles around. Under his brush, ordinary
letters became beautiful words—words of wisdom,
words of warning, or words that simply said which
door to use.

When he painted STOP, people stopped because the
sign looked so important. When he painted PLEASE
KEEP OFF THE GRASS, they kept off because the
sign was polite and sensible. When he painted

GOOD FOOD, they just naturally became hungry.

People thanked the signmaker and paid him well. But the kind old man never failed to say, "I couldn't have done it without Norman's help."

Norman was the signmaker's assistant. Each day after school he cut wood, mixed colors, and painted simple signs.

"Soon I will have a shop of my own," said Norman.

"Perhaps," answered the signmaker, "but not before you clean these brushes."

One day, after his work was done, Norman stood at a window over the sign shop and watched people. They stopped at the STOP sign. They entered at the ENTER sign. They ate under the GOOD FOOD sign.

"They do whatever the signs say!" said Norman to himself. "I wonder. . . ." He crept into the shop while the signmaker napped. With brush and board he painted a sign of his own.

Early the next morning he put up the sign, then ran back to his window to watch.

"No school?" muttered the principal. "How could I forget such a thing?"

"No one informed me," said the teacher.

"Hooray!" cheered the children, and everyone went home.

"This is great!" cried Norman. He looked around town for another idea. "Oh," he said at last, "there is something I have always wanted to do."

The following day Norman jumped from the top of the fountain in the park. As he swam, he thought to himself, *I can do lots of things with signs.* Ideas filled his head.

That afternoon when Norman went to work, the signmaker said, "I must drive to the next town and paint a large sign on a storefront. I'll return tomorrow evening, so please lock up the shop tonight."

As soon as the signmaker was gone, Norman started making signs. He painted for hours and hours and hours.

In the morning people discovered new signs all around town.

Norman watched it all
and laughed until tears came
to his eyes. But soon he saw
people becoming angry.

341

"The signmaker is playing tricks," they shouted. "He has made fools of us!"

The teacher tore down the NO SCHOOL TODAY sign. Suddenly people were tearing down all the signs— not just the new ones but every sign the signmaker had ever painted.

Then the real trouble started. Without store signs, shoppers became confused. Without stop signs, drivers didn't know when to stop. Without street signs, firemen became lost.

In the evening when the signmaker returned
from his work in the next town, he knew nothing of
Norman's tricks. An angry crowd of people met him at
the back door of his shop and chased him into
the woods.

As Norman watched, he suddenly realized that
without signs and without the signmaker, the town was
in danger.

"It's all my fault!" cried Norman, but no one
was listening.

Late that night the signmaker returned and saw a light on in his shop. Norman was feverishly painting.

While the town slept and the signmaker watched, Norman put up stop signs, shop signs, street signs, danger signs, and welcome signs; in and out signs, large and small signs, new and beautiful signs. He returned all his presents and cleared away the garbage at the grocery store. It was morning when he finished putting up his last sign for the entire town to see.

Then Norman packed his things and locked up the shop. But as he turned to go, he discovered the signmaker and all the townspeople gathered at the door.

"I know you're angry with me for what I did," said Norman with downcast eyes, "so I'm leaving."

"Oh, we were angry all right!" answered the school principal. "But we were also fools for obeying signs without thinking."

"You told us you are sorry," said the signmaker, "and you fixed your mistakes. So stay and work hard. One day this shop may be yours."

"Perhaps," answered Norman, hugging the old man, "but not before I finish cleaning those brushes."

Common Core State Standards

Literature 1. Ask and answer such questions as *who, what, where, when, why,* and *how* to demonstrate understanding of key details in a text. **Also Literature 7., Writing 3.**

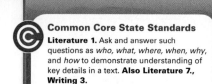

Envision It! Retell

READING STREET ONLINE
STORY SORT
www.ReadingStreet.com

Think Critically

1. What signs do you see in your community? How are they like the ones in the story? Text to World

2. This is a funny, entertaining story. What other message do you think the author might be trying to give you? Think Like an Author

3. What is the topic of this story? What is its main idea? Main Idea and Details

4. Look at the picture of the two men on page 341. Why are they holding their heads? Inferring

5. Look Back and Write

Look back at page 346. How does Norman fix the problems he caused? Provide evidence to support your answer.

Key Ideas and Details • Text Evidence

Meet the Author
Tedd Arnold

Once Tedd Arnold rode a bus through a town and noticed all the store signs. The signs were nice, and he thought about the person who painted them. The signmaker told people where to go. He controlled what the neighborhood looked like. Mr. Arnold said, "I began to wonder how else a signmaker might have control. Of course, I started thinking of silly signs that could control people and make them do goofy things. That's how the story got started!"

Read more books written or illustrated by Tedd Arnold.

No More Water in the Tub!

Tracks

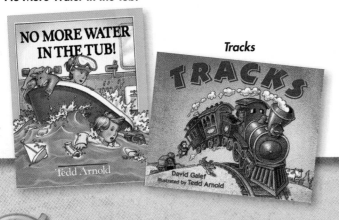

Use the *Reader's and Writer's Notebook* to record your independent reading.

Common Core State Standards

Writing 3. Write narratives in which they recount a well-elaborated event or short sequence of events, include details to describe actions, thoughts, and feelings, use temporal words to signal event order, and provide a sense of closure. **Also Language 2.c.**

Key Features of Humorous Fiction

- tells a funny story
- is about made-up people and events

READING STREET ONLINE
GRAMMAR JAMMER
www.ReadingStreet.com

Narrative

Humorous Fiction

Humorous fiction tells a funny story. The characters and events are make-believe. The student model on the next page is an example of humorous fiction.

Writing Prompt Think about funny stories that you have read or heard. Now write a humorous story.

Writer's Checklist

Remember, you should . . .

☑ tell about an event that is funny.

☑ write sentences that don't all begin alike.

☑ write contractions correctly.

The Talking Sandwich

Today I was ready to bite my sandwich. Then I heard, "Don't bite!" Wow! Was the sandwich talking?

"A sandwich can't talk!" I said.

"I'm not joking. You should give me to your sister."

The voice sounded like my sister! She was hiding behind a chair and talking!

**Genre
Humorous
Fiction**
The writer adds funny details.

Contractions combine two words:
I + am = I'm.

Writing Trait
These **sentences** begin different ways.

Conventions

Contractions

Remember A **contraction** puts two words together. Contractions include **I'm, she'll, you're, he's,** and others with pronouns. Contractions include words with *not* (**can't, isn't, won't**). A contraction has an **apostrophe** (').

351

Common Core State Standards
Informational Text 5. Know and use various text features (e.g., captions, bold print, subheadings, glossaries, indexes, electronic menus, icons) to locate key facts or information in a text efficiently.

21st Century Skills

Can you trust what you read on the Internet? You should always find out who wrote what you read. Can you believe that person? How can you tell? It is important to always check.

- The Internet has many Web sites that give information.

- You need to decide what is good information and what is not.

- Web sites you can count on often end in *.gov, .edu,* or *.org.*

- Web sites that end in *.com* must be checked carefully.

- Read "Helping Hand." Think about how you can decide whether an online source is a good one.

Helping Hand

The signmaker's assistant, Norman, learned about being responsible. You can do an Internet search to find out how you can help your neighbors. Use a search engine and type in the keyword *volunteer.* Here are two topics you might find listed. Which one would tell you about volunteer work? To choose, look carefully at both the source and the description.

This is a .*com* Web site. A .*com* site often sells things. It may or may not be a good source.

File   Edit   View   Favorites   Tools   Help

http://www.url.here

Show Your Colors T-shirts, bumper stickers, decals, and other items can show your loyalty to a group that you support.

Save the Whales!

Organizations Started by Kids
Think you're too young to start your own organization? Hmm . . . maybe you'll change your mind after seeing what these kids have done.

WE RECYCLE

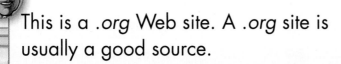

This is a .*org* Web site. A .*org* site is usually a good source.

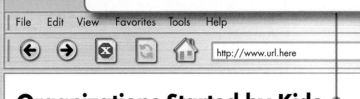

The link Organizations Started by Kids looks good to you. When you click on it, you get a list of other links. Here are some of them:

File   Edit   View   Favorites   Tools   Help

http://www.url.here

Organizations Started by Kids

Care Bags Foundation Annie Wignall, eleven years old

Grandma's Gifts Emily Douglas, nine years old

Kids For A Clean Environment (F.A.C.E.) Melissa Poe, nine years old

Kids Saving the Rain Forest Janine Licare Andrews and Aislin Livingstone, nine years old

Pennies to Protect Police Dogs Stacey Hillman, eleven years old

You may want to know more about these volunteer organizations. You decide to explore some of these links by clicking on them.

File   Edit   View   Favorites   Tools   Help

http://www.url.here

Kids For A Clean Environment (F.A.C.E.)

Kids F.A.C.E. is an environmental group. Kids from around the world belong to it. It was started in 1989 by nine-year-old Melissa Poe of Nashville, Tennessee. The club provides a way for children to protect nature. The club connects them with other children who share their concerns about environmental issues. Kids F.A.C.E. currently has 300,000 members.

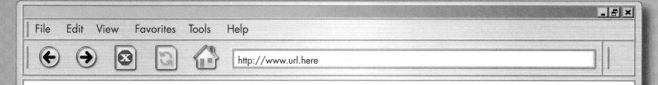

Pennies to Protect Police Dogs

Eleven-year-old Stacey Hillman started Pennies to Protect Police Dogs. She had read about police dogs and their dangerous jobs. One police dog had been shot on the job. The article mentioned that there were bulletproof vests for police dogs, but the vests cost a lot. Over the years, Pennies to Protect Police Dogs has raised more than $100,000. The group has outfitted more than 158 K-9 dogs with bulletproof vests.

After reading about both of these groups, you can decide which one might be best for you.

Common Core State Standards

Language 4. Determine or clarify the meaning of unknown and multiple-meaning words and phrases based on grade 2 reading and content, choosing flexibly from an array of strategies. **Also Foundational Skills 4.a., Speaking/Listening 1., 3.**

Let's Learn It!

Vocabulary

Suffixes

Word Structure A suffix is a word part added to the end of a word. The word part **-ful** is a suffix. The suffix **-ful** means "full of."

care   careful

Care is a base word. **Careful** is the word **care** plus the suffix **-ful.** **Careful** means "full of care."

Practice It! Add the suffix **-ful** to each word. Tell what the new word means.

cheer   doubt   help   pain

Fluency

Appropriate Phrasing

Group words into phrases as you read. Also pay attention to punctuation. Pause at commas. Stop at end punctuation such as periods and question marks. This will help you understand what you're reading.

Practice It! Read aloud pages 337–338 from *The Signmaker's Assistant* with a partner. Group words as you read. Do not read word-by-word. Pay attention to punctuation.

Listening and Speaking

Get Ready For Grade 3

Use formal language when speaking to the class.

Identify and Speak to Your Audience

You can use informal language, like slang, when speaking with friends or family. You should use formal language when speaking to the class. When you use formal language, you speak in complete sentences, and use proper conventions.

Practice It! Research information on an animal you like. Find two facts about the animal. Give a short report to the class. Remember to speak clearly and use formal language. Listen attentively while others give their reports.

Tips

Speaking . . .

• Use articles, like *an* and *the*, in your report.

• Use adverbs about manner, like *carefully* and *beautifully*, in your report.

Traditions

Are traditions and celebrations important in our lives?

Reading Street Online

www.ReadingStreet.com
- Big Question Video
- eSelections
- Envision It! Animations
- Story Sort

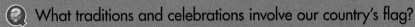

Oral Vocabulary

Let's Talk About

Sports Traditions

- Share information about boys and girls playing sports.

- Share ideas about how sports are an important tradition in our culture.

READING STREET ONLINE
CONCEPT TALK VIDEO
www.ReadingStreet.com

360

361

Let's **Think** About...

What do you already know about baseball?
Background Knowledge

Grandmama says there's
nothing like baseball.
The story goes. . . .

Josh Gibson once hit a baseball in Pittsburgh so hard that it didn't come down.

Let's **Think** About...

Could the story of Josh Gibson's hit really have happened?
Questioning

The next day he was playing in Philadelphia, and the ball dropped out of the sky, right into a fielder's glove. The umpire pointed at Josh and said, "You're out yesterday in Pittsburgh!"

Grandmama says her papa showed up on that same day, the day she was born, with a Louisville slugger and a smile. He said his new baby would make baseballs fly, just like Josh Gibson.

So Grandmama's papa threw balls to his baby girl in the early morning dew. Those summer days were like magic as the balls sailed away, sailed away, gone.

Let's **Think** About...

What is a Louisville Slugger? Look for clues in the pictures and story.
⊙ **Monitor and Clarify**

But girls in the forties didn't play baseball. They weren't supposed to take the field with the boys or have batting dreams.

So even when Grandmama got bigger, she still had to stand outside the fence and watch her cousin Danny and the Maple Grove All-Stars batting away.

Let's Think About...

Why didn't Grandmama play baseball with her cousin Danny? You can go back and reread the page.

◉ **Monitor and Clarify**

But every now and again, when the team was just practicing, they'd let Grandmama play too. Then Grandmama would step up to the plate, hit the ball, and watch it soar.

Grandmama says Danny would imagine he was playing with the Dodgers. But she was always Josh Gibson, playing for the Grays, wearing the team colors and hitting away.

Grandmama says she would play all day, with everybody saying she could do it all, hit, throw, and fly round the bases. "But too bad she's a girl. . . ."
Too bad she's a girl. . . .

Let's Think About...

Why do the boys say, "too bad she's a girl"?
Questioning

Until . . . two days, hot days after the Fourth of July, Danny hurt his arm sliding into second, and there were only eight All-Stars.

That afternoon the team looked to Grandmama—pink dress with a white bow, and Danny's baseball shoes.

And Grandmama says as she went to the plate she remembered . . .

Let's **Think** About...

Do you think Grandmama will get a hit? Why do you think so? Read to find out.
Predict

baseball has always been early morning dew and sunlight, hitting balls with her papa, and standing behind the fence, watching the boys play.

Let's Think About...

How did baseball change for Grandmama?

⊙ Monitor and Clarify

377

Let's **Think** About...

What does the picture tell you about how Grandmama did? **Inferring**

378

The story goes . . .
Grandmama hit the ball a mile
that day, caught anything that
was thrown, and did everything
else—just like Josh Gibson.

Let's Think About...

Knowing how
Grandmama
played, what kind
of player do you
think Josh Gibson
was? **Inferring**

379

As she hands the ball to me she says, "There's nothing like baseball, baby, and I couldn't help but love it, especially that one time I got to hear the cheers, hear all the cheers, while stealing home."

Let's **Think** About...

Grandmama's papa taught her about baseball. How is she doing the same thing now?

Monitor and Clarify

Common Core State Standards

Literature 1. Ask and answer such questions as *who, what, where, when, why,* and *how* to demonstrate understanding of key details in a text. **Also Literature 7., Writing 3.**

Envision It! | Retell

**READING STREET ONLINE
STORY SORT**
www.ReadingStreet.com

Think Critically

1. Grandmama liked playing baseball. Do you play baseball or another sport? Tell about it. Text to Self

2. Why do you think the author wrote about Grandmama and baseball? Think Like an Author

3. Look at page 373. Grandmama could not play baseball on the Maple Grove All-Stars because she was a girl. How is that different from girls' sports today? Compare and Contrast

4. Think of a question about Grandmama playing baseball. Reread to find the answer. What clues helped you answer the question? Monitor and Clarify

5. Look Back and Write Look back at page 379. How can a girl play baseball just like Josh Gibson? Provide evidence to support your answer.

Key Ideas and Details • Text Evidence

Meet the Author

Angela Johnson

Angela Johnson has written many great stories. Childhood memories of her father's baseball games inspired *Just Like Josh Gibson*. She says, "I remember the smell of the glove oil, the sound the bats made as the players tapped them on home plate, and the hot dogs I couldn't get enough of. Baseball is a wonderful memory for me. I wanted to write a book about it being a memory for another little girl."

Ms. Johnson recently won an important award to help her continue to write her wonderful stories.

Read two more books by Angela Johnson.

Violet's Music

Do Like Kyla

Reading Log

Use the *Reader's and Writer's Notebook* to record your independent reading.

Common Core State Standards

Writing 3. Write narratives in which they recount a well-elaborated event or short sequence of events, include details to describe actions, thoughts, and feelings, use temporal words to signal event order, and provide a sense of closure. **Also Language 2., 2.a.**

Narrative

Realistic Fiction

Realistic fiction tells about made-up events that could really happen. The student model on the next page is an example of realistic fiction.

Writing Prompt Think about one of your favorite sports heroes. Now write a story about a character who wants to be like that sports figure.

Let's Write It!

Key Features of Realistic Fiction

- characters and the setting seem real
- characters do things that could really happen

READING STREET ONLINE
GRAMMAR JAMMER
www.ReadingStreet.com

Writer's Checklist

Remember, you should . . .
- ✓ include events that could really happen.
- ✓ include a strong ending.
- ✓ use capital letters correctly.

384

The Walter Payton Fan

Grandma told Mark about Walter Payton. Payton played football years ago. Mark read a book about him.

Ever since then, Mark wanted to be a good runner like Walter Payton.

Last Thanksgiving, Mark played football with his brothers. He scored the winning touchdown.

Now Grandma smiles and calls Mark "Mr. Payton."

Genre Realistic fiction has events that could really happen.

The writer has **capitalized** the name of a holiday.

Writing Trait Organization The writer included an interesting ending.

Conventions

Using Capital Letters

Days of the week, **months,** and **holidays** begin with capital letters. **Titles** for people begin with capital letters. **Mr.** Lee played ball on the **Fourth of July**.

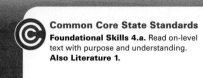
Common Core State Standards
Foundational Skills 4.a. Read on-level text with purpose and understanding. **Also Literature 1.**

Genre
Expository Text

- Expository text explains an object or idea.
- Expository text gives facts.
- Expository text may have graphic features.
- Read "How Baseball Began." Watch for facts and other elements that show this is expository text.

How Baseball Began

by Tammy Terry

illustrated by Clint Hansen

Baseball is called the national pastime of the United States. Hundreds of games are played and watched every spring and summer. But have you ever wondered how baseball began?

Who Invented It?

Well, no one knows for sure who invented the game. Many people believe that a man named Abner Doubleday invented baseball in 1839 in Cooperstown, New York.

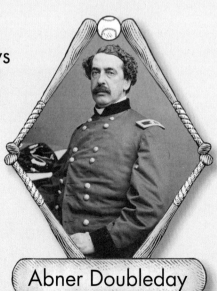

Abner Doubleday

In rounders, players threw the ball at runners. If a runner got hit, he was out.

Baseball probably developed from the English game of the 1600s called "rounders."

Settlers living in America played rounders in the 1700s. They also called the game "town ball" and "base ball." Rules of the game varied from place to place. Over the years, the game of rounders became the game we now call baseball. One of the biggest differences between the two games is in how a runner is put out.

In baseball, players tag runners to put them out.

Let's Think About...

Who do many people say invented baseball?
Expository Text

Let's Think About...

What is the main idea of this paragraph?
Expository Text

Players and Teams

The first official baseball game was played in Hoboken, New Jersey, on June 19, 1846. The New York Nine beat the Knickerbockers 23–1. More people became fans of the sport as more games were played.

In 1869, the Cincinnati Red Stockings became the first baseball team to get paid to play baseball. They won every game they played that year. Support for baseball continued to grow. More professional teams were formed. In 1876, eight teams joined to form the National League. The American League began in 1900 with eight teams.

Let's **Think** About...

What information can you learn about the two leagues from these charts?
Expository Text

YEAR	LEAGUE	TEAMS							
1876	National	⚾	⚾	⚾	⚾	⚾	⚾	⚾	⚾
1900	American	⚾	⚾	⚾	⚾	⚾	⚾	⚾	⚾

Today, sixteen teams play in the National League. There are fourteen teams in the American League.

YEAR	LEAGUE	TEAMS
2009	National	⚾⚾⚾⚾⚾⚾⚾⚾ ⚾⚾⚾⚾⚾⚾⚾⚾
2009	American	⚾⚾⚾⚾⚾⚾⚾⚾ ⚾⚾⚾⚾⚾⚾

They play in cities across the United States **(1)** and Canada **(2)**. Each year, millions of people go to baseball games, watch the games on TV, and read about the teams in newspapers. The sport has spread throughout the world, and baseball is now played in countries such as Japan **(3)**, Italy **(4)**, and South Africa **(5)**.

Let's **Think** About...

Reading Across Texts Use what you read in this article to figure out how long after the "invention" of baseball by Abner Doubleday it was that Grandmama played baseball.

Writing Across Texts Make a time line to show the important dates in baseball history. Be sure to include the time when Grandmama played.

389

Common Core State Standards
Foundational Skills 4.b. Read on-level text orally with accuracy, appropriate rate, and expression on successive readings. **Also Speaking/Listening 3., 6., Language 4.a.**

Let's Learn It!

**READING STREET ONLINE
ONLINE STUDENT EDITION
www.ReadingStreet.com**

Vocabulary

Homophones

Context Clues Homophones are words that sound alike but have different spellings and meanings. Use the context to understand the meaning of a homophone.

The boat has a large **sail**.
The store had jackets on **sale**.

Practice It! Use the context to tell the meaning of each homophone.

1. A hare looks very much like a rabbit. She is wearing her hair in a ponytail.

2. I heard a loud noise when the plane took off. A herd of elephants is at the water hole.

Fluency

Accuracy and Appropriate Rate

Read with accuracy. Read the words you see. Do not omit or add words. Read at a comfortable pace. Read at the same pace as you speak.

Practice It! Read the text below to a partner.

1. Kim wants to be an airline pilot.

2. Jamal wants to be a racecar driver.

390

Get Ready For Grade 3

Use clear and specific vocabulary words when you give an oral report.

Use Vocabulary to Express Ideas and Establish Tone

When giving an oral report, use clear and specific vocabulary to express ideas and establish tone. Choose your words carefully for reports. Specific words can make your meaning clear. For example, if you want to tell about a cherry tree, use the word *cherry*. Do not say fruit tree. When you use specific words, your listeners will know exactly what you mean. The words you choose can also let listeners know how you feel.

Sometimes when you are listening, you may not understand a word. You may not understand what a speaker means. Ask questions. The answers will help you understand the speaker's message.

Practice It! What activity do you like to do when you are not in school? Prepare a report. Tell the class about something you enjoy doing outside of school. Be sure to use common nouns correctly in your report. Remember to use formal language when giving your report. When others give their reports listen carefully. Ask questions if you do not understand.

Common Core State Standards

Language 6. Use words and phrases acquired through conversations, reading and being read to, and responding to texts, including using adjectives and adverbs to describe (e.g., *When other kids are happy that makes me happy*). **Also Speaking/Listening 1.**

Oral Vocabulary

Let's Talk About

The American Flag

- Share information about the Fourth of July and the Pledge of Allegiance.

- Share ideas about the National Anthem.

READING STREET ONLINE
CONCEPT TALK VIDEO
www.ReadingStreet.com

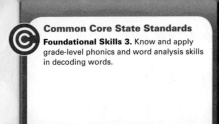

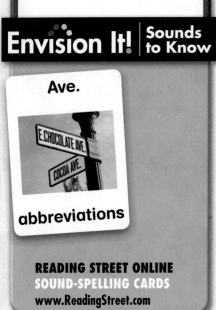

Phonics

Abbreviations

Words I Can Blend

Mr.
Ave.
Dr.
Feb.
Mon.

Sentences I Can Read

1. Mr. Jones lives at 235 Elm Ave.

2. I will see Dr. Lopez on Feb. 21.

3. Our last day of school is Mon., June 8.

I Can Read!

From: Ms. Sophie Martin

Subject: Oct. 14 party at 320 S. Main Ave.

Date: Thur., Sept. 29

To: Mrs. Grace Timmons; Dr. Abby Gomez;
Mr. Albert Soto Jr.; Ms. Susan Nelson

Dear Friends,

Mrs. Wilson and her class at Big Hollow School
are grateful to you. Without your help, our new
playground would not have been built. Please come
to a party to celebrate its grand opening. The party
will be held at 320 S. Main Ave., on Fri., Oct. 14,
from 1:00 P.M. until 3:00 P.M.
We would love to see you there.

You've learned

 Abbreviations

Common Core State Standards
Informational Text 6. Identify the main purpose of a text, including what the author wants to answer, explain, or describe.

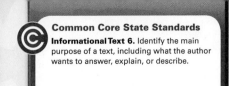

Skill

Strategy

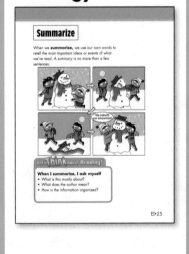

READING STREET ONLINE
ENVISION IT! ANIMATIONS
www.ReadingStreet.com

Comprehension Skill

Author's Purpose

- An author has a purpose, or reason, for writing.

- An author might write to entertain, to describe, or to explain.

- As you read "Flags," use a chart like this to identify the topic and explain the author's purpose.

Topic	Author's Purpose

Comprehension Strategy

Summarize

A summary is a brief retelling of a paragraph or a story. You summarize by telling only the most important ideas in your own words. Summarizing as you read can help you remember main events. It is a strategy that good readers use to check their understanding.

Flags

A flag is a piece of cloth. But it is much more. A flag is a symbol. It can stand for a country.

The flags of Canada, the United States, and Mexico use different colors and symbols.

A flag sends a message. Each color and picture on a flag tells something. The color red stands for courage. The color white stands for peace. The color blue stands for freedom. The flags of the United States, France, and Laos are red, white, and blue.

Strategy Summarize this paragraph in your own words.

Many flags have pictures. A picture of an eagle might stand for freedom. The flags of Egypt and Ecuador each have an eagle on them. Other flags, like the U.S. flag, have stars. The flag of China has five stars. The flag of Ghana has one big star. The Turkish flag has a star and the shape of the moon.

Skill Explain why the author wrote this text.

Your Turn!

Need a Review? See the *Envision It! Handbook* for additional help with author's purpose and summarize.

Ready to Try It? As you read *Red, White, and Blue*, use what you learned to help you understand the text.

Common Core State Standards

Language 4. Determine or clarify the meaning of unknown and multiple-meaning words and phrases based on grade 2 reading and content, choosing flexibly from an array of strategies. **Also Language 4.a.**

America

birthday

stars

flag

freedom

nicknames

stripes

Vocabulary Strategy for

Multiple-Meaning Words

Context Clues While reading, you may come across a word that has more than one meaning. For example, *bat* means "a stick used to hit a ball." *Bat* also means "a flying animal." You can use context clues to determine the relevant meaning.

1. Try the meaning you know. Does it make sense? If not, the word may have more than one meaning.

2. Read on and look at the nearby words. Can you figure out the meaning from the context?

3. Try the new meaning in a sentence. Does it make sense?

Read "America's Flag." Use context clues to find the relevant meaning of the multiple-meaning words.

Words to Write Reread "America's Flag." Write about what the flag means to you. Use words from the *Words to Know* list.

AMERICA'S FLAG

★ ★

We call it the Red, White, and Blue. We call it the Stars and Stripes too. These are nicknames for the American flag. You can probably guess why people call the flag by those names. Look at the picture of the flag. What colors do you see? You see red, white, and blue. What patterns do you see? You see stars and stripes.

People hang the flag outside their homes on special holidays such as the Fourth of July. That is our country's birthday.

On that day long ago, the American colonies declared their freedom from England. But you don't have to wait for a holiday. You can fly your flag anytime you want. When you look at it, think of what it stands for—America and freedom.

Your Turn!

❚❚ Need a Review? For more help with context clues and multiple-meaning words, see *Words!* on pp. W•7 and W•10.

▶ Ready to Try It? Read *Red, White, and Blue* on pp. 400–417.

Red, White, and Blue

★ ★ ★ ★ ★ ★ The Story of ★ ★ ★ ★ ★ ★
THE AMERICAN FLAG

★ ★ ★ ★ ★ ★ ★ BY ★ ★ ★ ★ ★ ★ ★
John Herman

ILLUSTRATED BY
Shannan Stirnweiss

Genre

Informational Text often gives facts about real people, places, and events that reflect history or the traditions of communities. Look for facts as you read.

Question of the Week

What traditions and celebrations involve our country's flag?

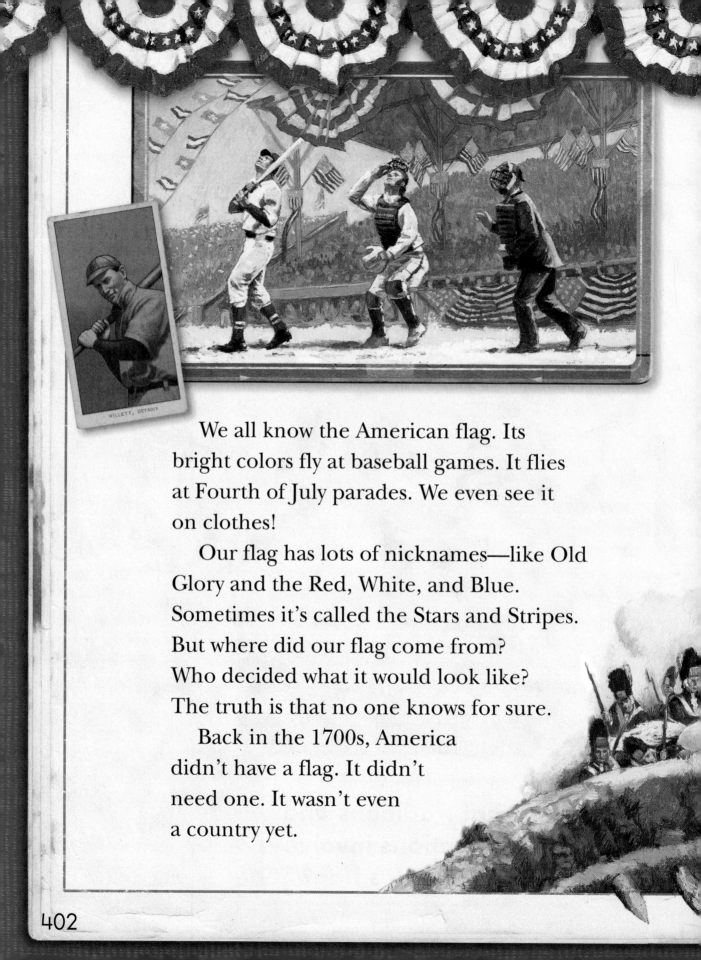

We all know the American flag. Its bright colors fly at baseball games. It flies at Fourth of July parades. We even see it on clothes!

Our flag has lots of nicknames—like Old Glory and the Red, White, and Blue. Sometimes it's called the Stars and Stripes. But where did our flag come from? Who decided what it would look like? The truth is that no one knows for sure.

Back in the 1700s, America didn't have a flag. It didn't need one. It wasn't even a country yet.

It was just thirteen colonies.
The colonies belonged to England.
The English flag flew in towns
from New Hampshire
to Georgia.

But as time went on, the
thirteen colonies didn't
want to belong to England
anymore. Americans
decided to fight for
their freedom.

A war began. It was the
American Revolution. Now a new flag
was needed—an American flag.

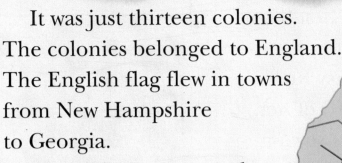

The original
13 American
colonies

New Hampshire
Massachusetts
Rhode Island
Connecticut
New York
New Jersey
Pennsylvania
Delaware
Maryland
Virginia
North Carolina
South Carolina
Georgia

Who made our first flag? Some people say it was a woman named Betsy Ross. Maybe you've heard of her. Betsy Ross owned a sewing shop in Philadelphia. She was famous for her sewing.

The story is that one day a general came to see her. The general was George Washington. He was the head of the American army.

General Washington wanted a new flag. It would make his soldiers feel like a real army fighting for a real country.

He wanted Betsy Ross to make this flag. He drew a picture of what he wanted.

Betsy Ross

George Washington

First American flag

Betsy Ross made some changes. Then she showed the picture to General Washington. He liked it!

Betsy Ross sewed the flag. And that was the very first Stars and Stripes.

That is the story—and it's a good one. But is it true? Betsy Ross's grandson said it was. He said that Betsy told him the story when he was a little boy and she was an old woman of eighty-four. But there is no proof for this story. So what do we know *for sure*?

We know that during the Revolution the colonists used lots of different flags.

Flags from the Revolutionary War

But once the colonies became the United States of America, the country needed *one* flag—the same flag for everybody.

So on June 14, 1777, a decision was made. The flag was going to have thirteen red and white stripes. The flag was also going to have thirteen white stars on a blue background, one for each of the thirteen colonies. Now the United States had a flag.

Congress had picked the colors and the stars and stripes. But Congress did not say where the stars and stripes had to go. So the flag still did not always look the same!

People could put them any way they liked. Sometimes the stripes were up and down, like this.

Sometimes the stars were in a circle, like this.

But nobody minded. Up and down or side to side, the stars and stripes still stood for the United States.

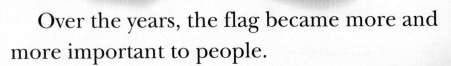

Over the years, the flag became more and more important to people.

In 1812, the United States was at war with England again. British soldiers came to America. They sailed up our rivers. They marched down our streets. They even burned down the White House—the home of the President.

Flag from battle at Fort McHenry

On the night of September 13, 1814, British soldiers bombed a fort in Maryland. All that night a man watched the fighting. His name was Francis Scott Key. He was afraid. What if the American soldiers in the fort gave up?

But in the early morning light, he saw the Stars and Stripes. It was still flying above the fort! He knew American soldiers had won the battle.

Key felt very proud. He wrote a poem about the flag on the fort. The poem was "The Star-Spangled Banner." Later the poem was put to music. This song about our flag became a song for our whole country.

Francis Scott Key

The flag that Francis Scott Key saw had fifteen stripes and fifteen stars. Why? Because by then there were two more states—Vermont and Kentucky.

American flag in 1814

First Fifteen American States

Vermont

Kentucky

New Hampshire
Massachusetts
Rhode Island
Connecticut
New York
New Jersey
Pennsylvania
Delaware
Maryland
Virginia
North Carolina
South Carolina
Georgia

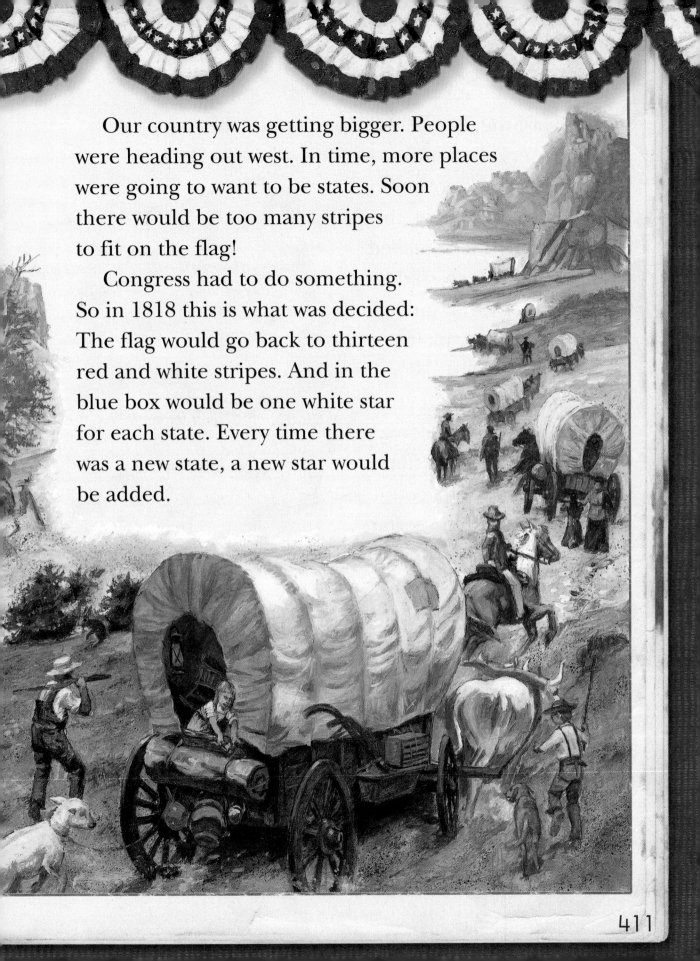

Our country was getting bigger. People were heading out west. In time, more places were going to want to be states. Soon there would be too many stripes to fit on the flag!

Congress had to do something. So in 1818 this is what was decided: The flag would go back to thirteen red and white stripes. And in the blue box would be one white star for each state. Every time there was a new state, a new star would be added.

At last the Stars and Stripes looked the same everywhere it flew. And Americans were proud of their flag. They took the flag with them as they moved west. The flag crossed the Mississippi River and the great grassy plains and the Rocky Mountains. It made it all the way to California.

More and more states were added to the country. And more and more stars were added to the flag. By 1837, there were twenty-six stars on the flag. By 1850, there were thirty-one.

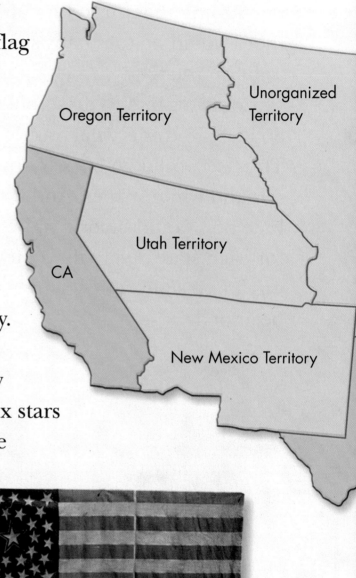

Oregon Territory

Unorganized Territory

Utah Territory

CA

New Mexico Territory

American flag in 1850

The United States in 1850

This map shows all the states as of 1850.

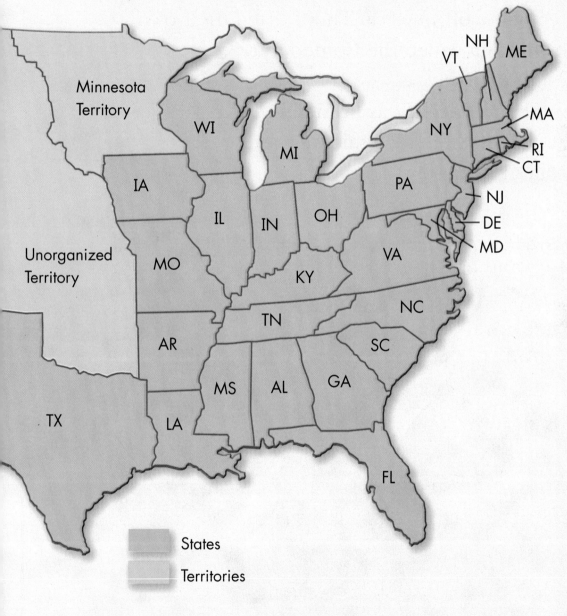

Minnesota Territory

Unorganized Territory

WI

MI

IA

IL

IN

OH

MO

KY

TN

AR

MS

AL

GA

LA

TX

FL

SC

NC

VA

PA

NY

VT

NH

ME

MA

RI

CT

NJ

DE

MD

States

Territories

One country. One flag. But then in 1861, something happened. Our country split in two. Eleven states in the South broke away from the United States of America. They started their own country. It was called the Confederate States of America.

Abraham Lincoln was President of the United States. He said *all* the states had to stay together.

President
Abraham Lincoln

War broke out—the Civil War. It was a very sad time in the history of our country.

The eleven southern states stopped flying the Stars and Stripes. They had their own flag.

In the North, some people wanted eleven stars taken off the Stars and Stripes. But Abraham Lincoln would not do that. He said the states would get back together. He was right. The Civil War ended in 1865. The North won. And the United States was one country under one flag again.

On June 14, 1877, the flag had a birthday—a big one. It was 100 years old. All across the country, people had picnics and parties and parades. June 14 became a holiday—Flag Day.

Today our flag has fifty stars for the fifty United States of America. Some flags are huge. One weighs 500 pounds! It is flown every Fourth of July from the George Washington Bridge.

The American flag flies in towns and cities from coast to coast.

And that's not all. In 1969, two American astronauts were the first people ever to land on the moon. The astronauts took lots of moon rocks back to Earth. They also left something on the moon . . . the Stars and Stripes.

And do you know what? Our flag is still flying there!

Envision It! Retell

The United States in 1850

READING STREET ONLINE
STORY SORT
www.ReadingStreet.com

Think Critically

1. Where in your community might you see the flag flying, based on what you learned in the text? Text to World

2. Why do you think the author wrote about the American flag?

   Think Like an Author

3. Why did the author show flags from the Revolution on page 405?

   Author's Purpose

4. Summarize what you have learned about the design of the flag.

   Summarize

5. **Look Back and Write** Look back at page 409. Why did Francis Scott Key write "The Star-Spangled Banner"? Provide evidence to support your answer.

   Key Ideas and Details • Text Evidence

Meet the Author
John Herman

John Herman grew up near New York City. He knew he wanted to be a writer when he was twelve years old. Now he writes books for adults, teenagers, and children.

Mr. Herman likes to make up stories. *Red, White, and Blue* gave him a chance to write about real events. He loves reading about American history, so this was a new thing for him to try. He hopes to write more books like this in the future!

Read more books about the American flag.

The Flag We Love
by Pam Muñoz Ryan

Betsy Ross
by Alexandra Wallner

Use the *Reader's and Writer's Notebook* to record your independent reading.

Common Core State Standards

Writing 3. Write narratives in which they recount a well-elaborated event or short sequence of events, include details to describe actions, thoughts, and feelings, use temporal words to signal event order, and provide a sense of closure. **Also Language 2.**

Key Features of a Descriptive Poem or Song

- has carefully chosen words arranged in lines

- describes something and may have rhymes

- A song is like a poem that people sing.

READING STREET ONLINE
GRAMMAR JAMMER
www.ReadingStreet.com

Descriptive

Descriptive Poem or Song

A descriptive poem or song describes something. It may tell how someone feels too. Many poems and songs have words that rhyme. The student model on the next page is an example of a descriptive poem.

Writing Prompt Think about American symbols and traditions. Now write a poem about one of those symbols or traditions.

Writer's Checklist

Remember, you should . . .

✓ include words that describe.

✓ express your interest in the topic.

✓ use sentence punctuation and quotation marks correctly.

The Statue of Liberty

The Statue of Liberty is so grand.
She welcomes people to our land.
She holds her torch of light so high.
It looks like it could touch the blue sky.
She seems to say, "Come in and be free."
She is a great symbol of our country.

Genre This **descriptive poem** has words that rhyme and words that describe.

Writing Trait Voice The writer expresses feelings about the topic.

The writer uses **quotation marks** to show spoken words.

Conventions

Using Quotation Marks

Quotation marks (" ") show the beginning and end of the words someone says. A word such as *said* and the speaker's name are not inside the quotation marks. Place a period in a quotation inside the marks.

421

Social Studies in Reading

Genre
Poetry (Song)

- A song is a lyric poem set to music. Poetry shows lines of words that have rhythm.

- Poetry often rhymes.

- Poetry may tell about what the poet senses and feels.

- Read "You're a Grand Old Flag." As you read, think about how the songwriter feels about the American flag.

- Songs often use words that have different meanings from their ordinary meanings. Find the phrase "Ev'ry heart beats true." Is this the literal, or real, meaning of the words? Or do the words mean something else?

You're a Grand Old Flag

by George M. Cohan

You're a grand old flag,
You're a high flying flag
And forever in peace may
   you wave.
You're the emblem of the
   land I love.
The home of the free and
   the brave.

Ev'ry heart beats true
'Neath the red, white, and blue,
Where there's never a boast
   or brag.
Should auld acquaintance
   be forgot,
Keep your eye on the grand
   old flag.

422

Let's **Think** About...

How do the words create a **rhythm**? Find the words that **rhyme**.

Let's **Think** About...

Reading Across Texts "You're a Grand Old Flag" is one song about the flag of the United States. What other song about the flag did you read about in *Red, White, and Blue*?

Writing Across Texts Make a list of other traditional songs that you know.

423

Common Core State Standards
Foundational Skills 4.b. Read on-level text orally with accuracy, appropriate rate, and expression on successive readings. **Also Speaking/Listening 1., Language 4., 4.a.**

Let's Learn It!

READING STREET ONLINE
ONLINE STUDENT EDITION
www.ReadingStreet.com

Vocabulary

Multiple-Meaning Words

Context Clues A multiple-meaning word is a word that has more than one meaning. You can use context clues to determine what the relevant meaning is.

Practice It! Read each sentence. Choose the meaning of the bold word.

1. The boat started to **sink**.
   go under water
   a small tub with a drain

2. **Fall** is my favorite season.
   drop or come down   autumn

Fluency

Read with Accuracy

Be sure you read every word. Blend the sounds to read new words. Ask yourself if it is a word you know. Check the new word in the sentence to see if it makes sense.

Practice It! Choose a page from *Red, White, and Blue*. Read the page aloud to a partner. Check each other's understanding of the text.

424

Listening and Speaking

Share how ads use facts and opinions to sell goods.

Evaluate Advertisements

Companies use advertisements to sell their goods. You can see the ads on the Internet and television. You can see them in magazines and newspapers. Look at some ads. What do ads tell you about a product? Do they tell you what the product does? Do they say that everyone wants the product? Decide whether the ad gives mostly facts or mostly opinions.

Practice It! Work in groups. Look on the Internet or in a magazine for an ad. Write what the ad is for. Write what facts and opinions you find. Then share the information and your ideas with the class. Remember to speak clearly and use specific words. Remember to pay attention to others when they speak.

Tips

- Show the class a copy of your ad and point out its graphics and words.

- Speak at an appropriate pace.

- Use proper conventions of language.

Common Core State Standards

Language 6. Use words and phrases acquired through conversations, reading and being read to, and responding to texts, including using adjectives and adverbs to describe (e.g., *When other kids are happy that makes me happy*). **Also Speaking/Listening 1.**

Oral Vocabulary

Let's Talk About

Family Celebrations

- Share information about cultural traditions and certain activities.

- Share ideas about special foods.

READING STREET ONLINE
CONCEPT TALK VIDEO
www.ReadingStreet.com

427

Common Core State Standards
Foundational Skills 3. Know and apply
grade-level phonics and word analysis skills
in decoding words.

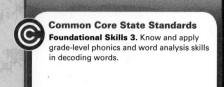

lotion

-tion

onion

-ion

furniture

-ture

Phonics

Final Syllables *-tion, -ture, -ion*

Words I Can Blend

picture

station

question

fashion

future

Sentences I Can Read

1. A picture of that train is hanging in the station.

2. Can you answer my question about the latest fashion?

3. In the future James will ask for things he needs.

I Can Read!

Julie likes books! What kind of books? Julie likes all kinds. She would read a million books if she could. She reads fiction and nonfiction. She reads action stories and adventure stories. She reads math books about fractions and art books about sculpture. She even reads picture books. If you ask Julie a question about the book she liked most, she will tell you. The most exciting book she ever read was about creatures on a space station in the future.

You've learned

◉ Final Syllables *-tion, -ture, -ion*

Common Core State Standards

Literature 1. Ask and answer such questions as *who, what, where, when, why,* and *how* to demonstrate understanding of key details in a text.

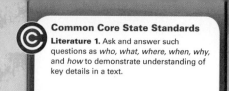

Skill

Strategy

READING STREET ONLINE
ENVISION IT! ANIMATIONS
www.ReadingStreet.com

Comprehension Skill

Draw Conclusions

- When you read, you can draw conclusions or figure out more about the characters and events in a story.

- Use evidence from the text to make conclusions.

- Use what you learned about draw conclusions and a diagram like the one below as you read "Empty Eggshells."

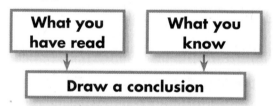

Comprehension Strategy

Questioning

Good readers ask themselves literal and relevant questions before, during, and after they read. As you read "Empty Eggshells," write your questions about the text on a sheet of paper. Look for evidence from the text to answer your questions. Share your questions with a partner.

Empty Eggshells

When Danny arrived early for Jorge's party, he saw a carton of eggs. But they were just empty eggshells, with a hole at the top. No egg inside.

"What do we do with these?" Danny asked.

"First, we will paint the eggshells. Next, we will fill each egg with tiny bits of paper," Jorge told him. "Then, my mother will glue paper over each hole."

Before the party, Jorge's father hid the painted eggs in the apartment. All the children went on an egg hunt, and all the eggs were found. Then—surprise! Jorge cracked one open over the top of Danny's head! The colored paper rained down! Danny laughed and laughed. Soon everyone at the party was cracking *cascarones* over one another's heads!

Strategy Ask a question here, such as "What does the family do with the empty eggshells first? What do they do next?"

Skill Here you can make a conclusion about Jorge and Danny. Do you think they are friends? How do you know?

Your Turn!

⏸ Need a Review? See the *Envision It! Handbook* for additional help with draw conclusions and questioning.

▶ Ready to Try It? As you read the story, use what you've learned to understand the text.

Common Core State Standards
Language 4.a. Use sentence-level context as a clue to the meaning of a word or phrase.

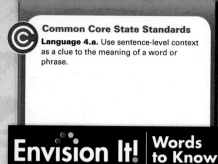
Vocabulary Strategy for

Words from Other Languages

Context Clues When you read, you may come to a word from another language. These words are sometimes in slanted type, or italics. If you do not know the word, you can sometimes learn its meaning from the context.

1. Look at the new word.

2. Use the context to determine the new word's relevant meaning.

3. Try the meaning of the word in the sentence. Does it make sense?

Read "A Party and a Present." Look for Spanish words. Use the context to figure out the relevant meaning of each word.

Words to Write Reread "A Party and a Present." Write sentences about a special gift you can give to someone. Use words from the *Words to Know* list.

A Party and a Present

Is someone you know having a birthday soon? Is he or she having a party, or a *fiesta*? What will you give that person? It is not hard to think of a present. Ask yourself what the person likes. What is his or her favorite game? Does he or she have a favorite hobby? favorite color? favorite food? See if the answers give you an idea.

You do not have to break your piggy bank to buy a present. Buy flowers at the grocery store. Find a basket or bowl at home. Arrange the flowers in it. This makes a nice present for your aunt, or *tía*.

Maybe this special person collects things such as baseball cards, photos, or rings. Decorate a box that has a lid. Find or draw pictures that match what the person collects.

Is your gift ready? Soon it will be *fiesta* time. Everyone will have fun. There will be games. There might even be a *piñata*!

Your Turn!

⏸ **Need a Review?** For more help with using context clues to determine the meaning of words from other languages, see *Words!* on p. W•7.

▷ **Ready to Try It?** Read *A Birthday Basket for Tía* on pp. 434–447.

A Birthday Basket for Tía

by Pat Mora

illustrated by Cecily Lang

434

Today is secret day. I curl my cat into my arms and say, "Ssshh, Chica. Can you keep our secret, silly cat?"

Today is special day. Today is my great-aunt's ninetieth birthday. Ten, twenty, thirty, forty, fifty, sixty, seventy, eighty, ninety. Ninety years old. *¡Noventa años!*

At breakfast Mamá asks, "What is today, Cecilia?" I say, "Special day. Birthday day."

Mamá is cooking for the surprise party. I smell beans bubbling on the stove. Mamá is cutting fruit—pineapple, watermelon, mangoes. I sit in the backyard and watch Chica chase butterflies. I hear bees bzzzzz.

I draw pictures in the sand with a stick. I draw a picture of my aunt, my *Tía*. I say, "Chica, what will we give Tía?"

437

Chica and I walk around the front yard and the backyard looking for a good present. We walk around the house. We look in Mamá's room. We look in my closet and drawers.

I say, "Chica, shall we give her my little pots, my piggy bank, my tin fish, my dancing puppet?"

I say, "Mamá, can Chica and I use this basket?"

Mamá asks, "Why, Cecilia?"

"It's a surprise for the surprise party," I answer. Chica jumps into the basket. "No," I say. "Not for you, silly cat. This is a birthday basket for Tía."

I put a book in the basket. When Tía comes to our house, she reads it to me. It's our favorite book. I sit close to her on the sofa. I smell her perfume. Sometimes Chica tries to read with us. She sits on the book. I say, "Silly cat. Books are not for sitting."

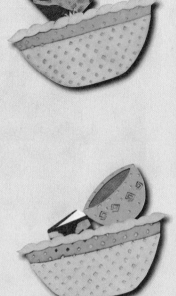

I put Tía's favorite mixing bowl on the book in the basket. Tía and I like to make *bizcochos*, sugary cookies for the family. Tía says, "Cecilia, help me stir the cookie dough." She says, "Cecilia, help me roll the cookie dough." When we take the warm cookies from the oven, Tía says, "Cecilia, you are a very good cook."

439

I put a flowerpot in the mixing bowl on the book in the basket. Tía and I like to grow flowers for the kitchen window. Chica likes to put her face in the flowers. "Silly cat," I say.

I put a teacup in the flowerpot that is in the mixing bowl on the book in the basket. When I'm sick, my aunt makes me hot mint tea, *hierbabuena*. She brings it to me in bed. She brings me a cookie too.

I put a red ball in the teacup that is in the flowerpot in the mixing bowl on the book in the basket. On warm days Tía sits outside and throws me the ball.

She says, "Cecilia, when I was a little girl in Mexico, my sisters and I played ball. We all wore long dresses and had long braids."

Chica and I go outside. I pick flowers to decorate Tía's basket. On summer days when I am swinging high up to the sky, Tía collects flowers for my room.

441

Mamá calls, "Cecilia, where are you?"

Chica and I run and hide our surprise.

I say, "Mamá, can you find the birthday basket
for Tía?"

Mamá looks under the table. She looks in the
refrigerator. She looks under my bed. She asks,
"Chica, where is the birthday basket?"

Chica rubs against my closet door. Mamá and
I laugh. I show her my surprise.

After my nap, Mamá and I fill a piñata with
candy. We fill the living room with balloons. I hum,
mmmmm, a little work song like the one Tía hums
when she sets the table or makes my bed. I help
Mamá set the table with flowers and tiny cakes.

"Here come the musicians," says Mamá. I open the front door. Our family and friends begin to arrive too.

I curl Chica into my arms. Then Mamá says, "Sshh, here comes Tía."

I rush to open the front door. "Tía! Tía!" I shout. She hugs me and says,

"Cecilia, *¿qué pasa?* What is this?"

"SURPRISE!" we all shout. "¡*Feliz cumpleaños!*
Happy birthday!" The musicians begin to play their
guitars and violins.

"Tía! Tía!" I say, "It's special day, birthday day! It's your ninetieth birthday surprise party!" Tía and I laugh.

445

I give her the birthday basket. Everyone gets close to see what's inside. Slowly Tía smells the flowers. She looks at me and smiles.

Then she takes the red ball out of the teacup and the teacup out of the flowerpot.

She pretends to take a sip of tea and we all laugh.

Carefully, Tía takes the flowerpot out of the bowl and the bowl off of the book. She doesn't say a word. She just stops and looks at me.

Then she takes our favorite book out of the basket.

And guess who jumps into the basket?

Chica. Everyone laughs.

Then the music starts and my aunt surprises me.
She takes my hands in hers. Without her cane, she
starts to dance with me.

Common Core State Standards

Literature 7. Use information gained from the illustrations and words in a print or digital text to demonstrate understanding of its characters, setting, or plot. **Also Literature 2., Writing 3.**

Envision It! | Retell

Think Critically

1. Cecilia puts six things in the birthday basket. Would you put the same six things in a gift basket? Explain.

Text to Self

2. Why do you think the author wrote a story about a birthday basket?

Think Like an Author

3. Pat Mora wrote this story and *The Night the Moon Fell*. How are the plots and settings of these two stories alike and different? Which story do you think she enjoyed writing more? Why? Draw Conclusions

4. Did anything in the story confuse you? What questions did you ask as you read? Questioning

5. Look Back and Write Look back at page 440. Why does Cecilia put a flowerpot and a teacup in the basket for Tía? Provide evidence to support your answer.

Key Ideas and Details • Text Evidence

Meet the Author

Pat Mora

Though Pat Mora grew up in Texas, she came from a home where both English and Spanish were spoken. When she started writing books, Ms. Mora realized she wanted to write about her experience as a Mexican American. "It was like opening a treasure chest," Ms. Mora says. "My whole Mexican heritage was something I could write about."

Ms. Mora tells students to write about what they love. She says, "The trick is how we bring everything that we are to the page—everything."

Read two more books by Pat Mora.

Tomás and the Library Lady

This Big Sky

Use the *Reader's and Writer's Notebook* to record your independent reading.

Key Features of an Invitation Letter

- asks someone to come to a planned event

- gives details about where and when the event will be

- has a greeting and a closing

READING STREET ONLINE
GRAMMAR JAMMER
www.ReadingStreet.com

Invitation Letter

An invitation letter asks someone to come to an event. The student model on the next page is an example of an invitation letter.

Writing Prompt Think about family parties and how to plan a family party. Write an invitation letter to invite a relative to an event.

Writer's Checklist

Remember, you should . . .
- ✓ write clear sentences to invite the person.
- ✓ begin the greeting and closing with a capital letter.
- ✓ use prepositional phrases correctly.

Dear Uncle Ed,

We are having a party to celebrate Luz coming home. It will be fun.

The day will be Sunday, June 24, 2011. The party will start at 1:00 in the afternoon. It will be at Grandma's house in La Porte.

Please come. We enjoy seeing you when you visit.

Your niece,

Briana

Genre
An **invitation letter** has a greeting and a closing.

Writing Trait Sentences
The writer uses words in an order that makes sense.

Writer uses **prepositions** correctly.

Conventions

Prepositions and Prepositional Phrases

A **preposition** is the first word in a prepositional phrase. Prepositions may tell where something is or when something happens. The words **on, at,** and **in** are prepositions.

451

Common Core State Standards

Informational Text 5. Know and use various text features (e.g., captions, bold print, subheadings, glossaries, indexes, electronic menus, icons) to locate key facts or information in a text efficiently.

21st Century Skills

A good directory is like a good friend. It will help you find what you need. Find the category you need. Then follow the links and read. Bookmark a good directory to save it.

- Online directories give links to Web sites about a topic you choose.

- A link is a special text feature of online text. Links are underlined or appear in a different color.

- Clicking on a link takes you to another Web site.

- Read "Family Traditions: Birthdays." Use the illustrations along with the text to learn how an online directory works.

Family Traditions: Birthdays

How can you find out more about birthdays? You can go to an Internet online directory. Here are some of the topics you might find listed there.

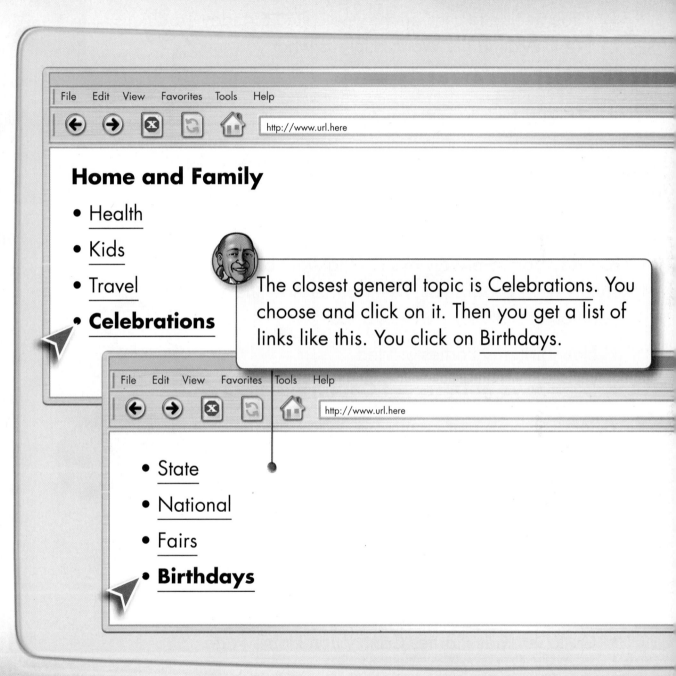

Home and Family

- Health
- Kids
- Travel
- **Celebrations**

The closest general topic is Celebrations. You choose and click on it. Then you get a list of links like this. You click on Birthdays.

- State
- National
- Fairs
- **Birthdays**

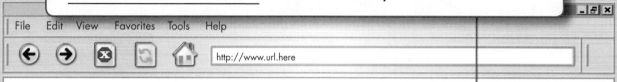

When you click on Birthdays, you get a list of Web sites. You decide to click on the one called Birthday Traditions from Around the World. Here is what you see:

File   Edit   View   Favorites   Tools   Help

http://www.url.here

Birthday Traditions from Around the World

Discover how the tradition of birthdays started. Find out how people in other countries celebrate birthdays.

Birthday parties are always the highlight of a child's year, but did you ever wonder how the tradition of birthday parties started?

- How Birthday Parties Started
- **Birthdays in Different Countries**
- Tell Us About Your Family's Birthday Traditions
- See a Listing of Birthday Party Places
- Find a Birthday Present
- Find Out What Famous People Share Your Birth Date
- Children's Book and Video Store
- Birthday-Related Products and Links
- Go to the Kids' Parties Connection Home Page

You click on the link Birthdays in Different Countries. You can read about some of these traditions on the next page.

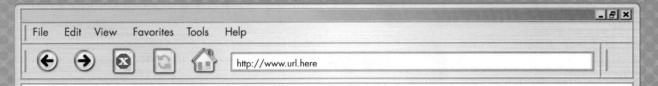

Birthdays in Different Countries

Canada—In some parts of Canada, birthday children get their noses greased for good luck. Greased noses make children too slippery for bad luck to catch them.

China—People are invited to lunch. Noodles are served to wish the birthday child a long life.

Cuba—The parties are similar to those in the United States. Food, decorations, gifts, piñatas, cake, candles, the "Happy Birthday" song, and games are included.

India—At school, the birthday child wears special clothing and passes out chocolates to the entire class.

Vietnam—Everyone's birthday is celebrated on New Year's Day, called Tet. The Vietnamese do not celebrate the exact day they were born. A baby turns one on Tet no matter when he or she was born that year.

Common Core State Standards
Foundational Skills 4.a. Read on-level
text with purpose and understanding.
Also Speaking/Listening 1.a., 3.,
Language 4.a.

Let's Learn It!

READING STREET ONLINE
ONLINE STUDENT EDITION
www.ReadingStreet.com

Vocabulary

Words from Other Languages

Context Clues Sometimes stories and articles have words that come from other languages. You can use the context around the word to determine its meaning.

Practice It! Find these words in *A Birthday Basket for Tía*. Use the context to determine their relevant meaning. Write a sentence with each word.

**bizcochos   hierbabuena
piñata   feliz cumpleaños**

Fluency

Appropriate Phrasing
When reading, look for groups of words that go together. Commas and periods often show how words are grouped. Be sure you understand what you're reading.

Practice It! Read the text aloud to a partner.

Yesterday, I took my dog for a walk to the dog park. When we came to the big pond, I let him play in the water. He jumped into the water and swam. Then he shook himself off, and we left.

Listening and Speaking

Think about your listeners' interests when preparing a descriptive report.

Listen to a Description

Listen carefully to descriptions. When preparing a description for an oral report, remember your listeners. Think about their interests. Ask yourself, "What will they like to hear?" Use sensory words in the description. Tell how something looks, feels, sounds, and smells. Then your listeners can visualize what you are describing. Listen carefully when others give a report. Try to visualize what the speakers are describing.

Practice It! Plan a report to describe an object or a story. As you prepare your description, think of sensory words you can use. Also think of prepositions and prepositional phrases you can use. Then give your report to the class. Listen to the reports other students give. Visualize what they are describing.

Tips

- Use sensory words so listeners can visualize what you are describing.

- Speak clearly and at an appropriate pace so listeners can hear and understand you.

Oral Vocabulary

Let's Talk About

Cowboys

- Share information about the hard work and the difficult working conditions.

- Share ideas about the protective clothing.

READING STREET ONLINE
CONCEPT TALK VIDEO
www.ReadingStreet.com

458

COWBOYS

by Lucille Recht Penner
illustrated by Ben Carter

Informational Text often gives facts about real people, places, and events that reflect history or the traditions of communities. Look for facts about cowboys.

459

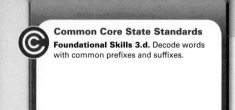

Envision It! | Sounds to Know

kindness

-ness

adorable

toothless

-able

-less

convertible

-ible

Phonics

🎯 Suffixes -ness, -less, -able, -ible

Words I Can Blend

comfortable

darkness

careless

reversible

seedless

Sentences I Can Read

1. Her sister felt comfortable walking in the darkness.

2. That was careless of him to leave his reversible jacket in the rain.

3. We enjoy eating seedless fruits.

I Can Read!

My family has a fondness for fresh fruit. Every fall we pick fruit at Benson Farms near our home. Dad and Mom tell us to check the fruit for ripeness and redness before we pick it. They remind us not to be careless with the fruit. Needless to say, my sister and I are very capable of picking countless pieces of spotless fruit. We stay at that farm until darkness sets in. With some sadness we head home. It is the end of an incredible day.

You've learned

● Suffixes -ness, -less, -able, -ible

Common Core State Standards

Informational Text 3. Describe the connection between a series of historical events, scientific ideas or concepts, or steps in technical procedures in a text. **Also Informational Text 2.**

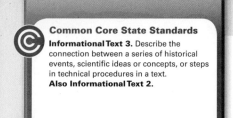

Envision It! | Skill Strategy

Skill

Strategy

Comprehension Skill

🎯 Sequence

- Sequence is the order of events in a story.

- Clue words such as *first, next, then,* and *finally* will help you describe the order of events in a text.

- Use what you learned about sequence and complete an organizer like this as you read "The Stagecoach Driver."

What happens first	
What happens next	
What happens last	

Comprehension Strategy

🎯 Text Structure

Text structure is the way a selection is organized. Many stories are organized in time order. They are organized to tell what happened at the beginning, middle, and end. You can use text structure to help you remember what the selection says, and to retell it.

THE STAGECOACH DRIVER

To start a trip, a driver helped the riders and checked the horses. First, the driver helped riders get on the stagecoach. He helped them load their cases and bags. Then, he checked the horses. He made sure they were ready for the trip. He checked the wheels too. Then, he would get on the stagecoach, and the trip began!

The stagecoach driver had to be careful. The trails and roads were muddy and rocky. He did not want the stagecoach to get stuck or tip over.

Finally, the stagecoach arrived after a long ride over the trail. The driver helped the riders off the stagecoach. He helped unload the cases and bags. Both the driver and the horses were tired after the trip. They needed to rest before the next trip.

Skill Describe what the stagecoach driver does before a trip. What are the clue words?

Strategy What steps does the driver take when the ride is over?

Your Turn!

❚❚ **Need a Review?** See the *Envision It! Handbook* for additional help with sequence and text structure.

▶ **Ready to Try It?** As you read *Cowboys*, use what you've learned to understand the text.

COWBOYS

Envision It! | **Words to Know**

cattle

cowboy

herd

campfire

galloped

railroad

trails

Vocabulary Strategy for

🎯 Unfamiliar Words

Context Clues When you come to a word you don't know while reading, what can you do? You can look for context clues around the word. This strategy can help you figure out the relevant meaning of the word.

1. Read the words and sentences around the word you don't know. Sometimes the author explains the word.

2. Use context clues to develop a meaning for the word.

3. Try that meaning in the sentence. Does it make sense?

Read "Like a Cowboy." Look for context clues to help you understand the meanings of the *Words to Know*.

Words to Write Reread "Like a Cowboy." Would you like to be a cowboy or cowgirl? Why or why not? Write a paragraph. Use words from the *Words to Know* list.

LIKE A COWBOY

What was it like to be a cowboy long ago? To find out, some people stay on a ranch. They ride horses, and they chase and rope cattle, or cows. At night around a campfire, they tell stories and sing songs. They even take a herd of cattle on a cattle drive.

Long ago, cowboys took herds of cattle on long cattle drives. They traveled on trails that ran from Texas to Kansas. From there, the railroad took the cattle to cities in the East. The trail was a thousand miles long. The cattle drive lasted for months.

The cattle drive at the ranch today lasts only a day or two. Still, the cattle drive gives people an idea of what it was like to be a cowboy. They can imagine how hard the cowboys worked on the trail. They can imagine how happy the cowboys were as they galloped into town after a long cattle drive.

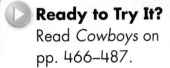

COWBOYS

Your Turn!

❚❚ Need a Review? For more help with using context clues to help you find the meanings of unfamiliar words, see *Words!* on p. W•7.

▷ Ready to Try It? Read *Cowboys* on pp. 466–487.

COWBOYS

by Lucille Recht Penner
illustrated by Ben Carter

Informational Text often gives facts about real people, places, and events that reflect history or the traditions of communities. Look for facts about cowboys.

Question of the Week

What can we learn about cowboy traditions?

467

If you were out west about a hundred years ago,
you might have heard a cowboy yelling—*ti yi yippy
yay!*—as he rode across the plains.

What was it like to be a cowboy way back then?
Cowboys lived on cattle ranches. A ranch had
a house for the rancher and his family, barns for
animals, and a bunkhouse where the cowboys slept.

The rancher owned thousands of cattle. They
wandered for miles looking for grass and water.

Twice a year, the cowboys drove all the cattle
together. This was called a roundup. The cowboys
counted the baby calves that had been born since
the last roundup. The biggest cattle were chosen to
sell at market.

A roundup was hard work. The cattle were wild and fast. They had long, sharp, dangerous horns. Cowboys called them Longhorns. If you made a Longhorn mad, it would charge at you. A cowboy didn't want to get close to an angry Longhorn.

So he made a loop in the end of his rope. Then he twirled it over his head and let it fly. When he caught the Longhorn, he could tell that it belonged to his ranch.

How could he tell? It was easy. Each rancher put a special mark called a brand on his cows. Baby calves didn't have brands, yet. They didn't need them. A baby calf always followed its mother.

Every ranch had its own name and its own brand. The Rocking Chair Ranch brand looked like a rocking chair. The Flying V Ranch brand looked like this: ⋃.

After the roundup was over, it was time to sell the Longhorns. That meant taking them to big market towns. Back then, there were no roads across the wide plains—only dusty trails that cattle had made with their hooves as they tramped along. Some trails were a thousand miles long! Since cattle could walk only fifteen miles a day, the long, hard trip often lasted months. It was called a trail drive. There was a lot to do to get ready.

At the beginning of a trail day, one cowboy rode out in front of the herd. "Come on, boys," he called

to the cattle. A few big Longhorns started after him. They bellowed and swung their heads from side to side. Other cattle followed, and soon they were all on their way.

Cattle didn't like so much walking. After a while, they wanted to turn around and go home. Cowboys rode up and down the sides of the herd to keep them in line. A few cowboys rode at the end of the herd to make sure no cattle were left behind.

It was hot on the trail. Cowboys wore hats
with wide brims to keep the sun out of their eyes.
When it rained, the brims made good umbrellas.
Around their necks, cowboys wore red bandannas.
When it got dusty, they pulled the bandannas
over their noses.

Leather leggings—called chaps—were tied over their pants to keep out thorns and cactus spines.

High leather boots kept out dirt and pebbles. Cowboy boots had handles called "mule ears." The cowboy grabbed the mule ears to pull his boots on.

What else did a cowboy need on his trail? A good horse. Cowboys spent the whole day on horseback. They rode little horses called cow ponies. A good cow pony was fearless. It could cross rough ground in the blackest night. It could swim a deep, wide river.

It could crash right through the bushes after a runaway cow. The cowboy had to hold on tight!

Every day the herd tramped the hot, dry plains. Two or three big steers were the leaders. They always walked in front. The cowboys got to know them well. They gave them pet names, like "Old Grumpy" and "Starface."

Cows could get in trouble. Sometimes one got stuck in the mud. The cowboy roped it and pulled it out. A cow might get hurt on the trail. A cowboy took care of that too.

At night the cowboys stopped to let the cattle eat, drink, and sleep. It was time for the cowboys to eat too. "Cookie" had a hot meal ready for them. That's what cowboys called the cook.

Cookie drove a special wagon called the chuckwagon. It had drawers for flour, salt, beans, and pots and pans. A water barrel was tied underneath.

Cookie gave every cowboy a big helping of biscuits, steak, gravy, and beans. He cooked the

same meal almost every night, but the cowboys didn't mind. It tasted good!

There were no tables or chairs, so the cowboys sat right on the ground. After dinner they played cards or read by the flickering light of the campfire. The nights were chilly and bright with stars.

But the cowboys didn't stay up late. They were tired. At bedtime, they just pulled off their boots and crawled into their bedrolls. A cowboy never wore pajamas. What about a pillow? He used his saddle.

Trail drives were dangerous. Many things could go wrong. The herd might stampede if there was a loud noise—like a sudden crash of thunder. A stampede was scary. Cattle ran wildly in all directions, rolling their eyes and bellowing with fear. The ground shook under them. The bravest cowboys galloped to the front of the herd. They had to make

the leaders turn. They shouted at them and fired their six shooters in the air. They tried to make the cattle run in a circle until they calmed down.

Sometimes they'd run into rustlers. A rustler was a cow thief. Rustlers hid behind rocks and jumped out at the cattle to make them stampede. While the cowboys were trying to catch the terrified cattle and calm them down, the rustlers drove off as many as they could.

When the herd came to a big river, the cowboys in front galloped right into the water. The cattle plunged in after them. The cattle swam mostly under water. Sometimes the cowboys could see only the tips of their black noses and their long white horns.

Most cowboys didn't know how to swim. If a cowboy fell into the water, he grabbed the horse's tail and held on tight until they reached shore.

Trail drives often went through Indian Territory. The Indians charged ten cents a head to let the cattle cross their land. If the cowboys didn't pay, there might be a fight. But usually the money was handed over and the herd plodded on.

484

At last, the noisy, dusty cattle stamped into a market town. The cowboys drove them into pens near the railroad tracks. Then they got their pay. It was time for fun!

What do you think most cowboys wanted first? A bath! The barber had a big tub in the back of the shop. For a dollar, you could soak and soak. A boy kept throwing in pails of hot water. Ahh-h-h! Next it was time for a shave, a haircut, and some new clothes.

Tonight, the cowboys would sleep in real beds and eat dinner at a real table. They would sing, dance, and have fun with their friends.

But soon they would be heading back to Longhorn country. There would be many more hot days in the saddle. There would be many more cold nights under the stars.

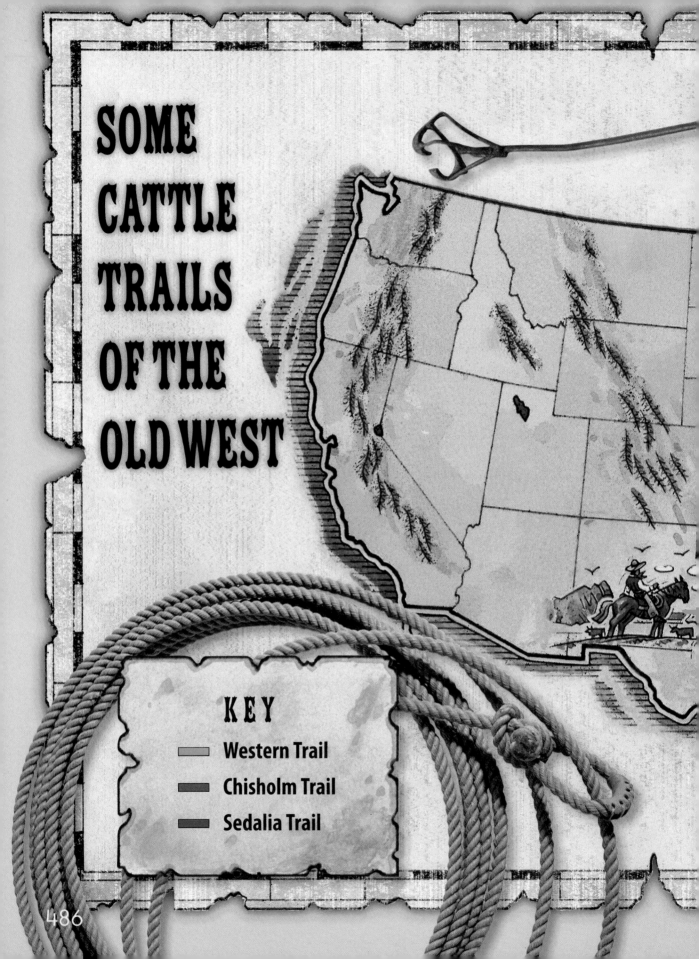

SOME CATTLE TRAILS OF THE OLD WEST

KEY

Western Trail

Chisholm Trail

Sedalia Trail

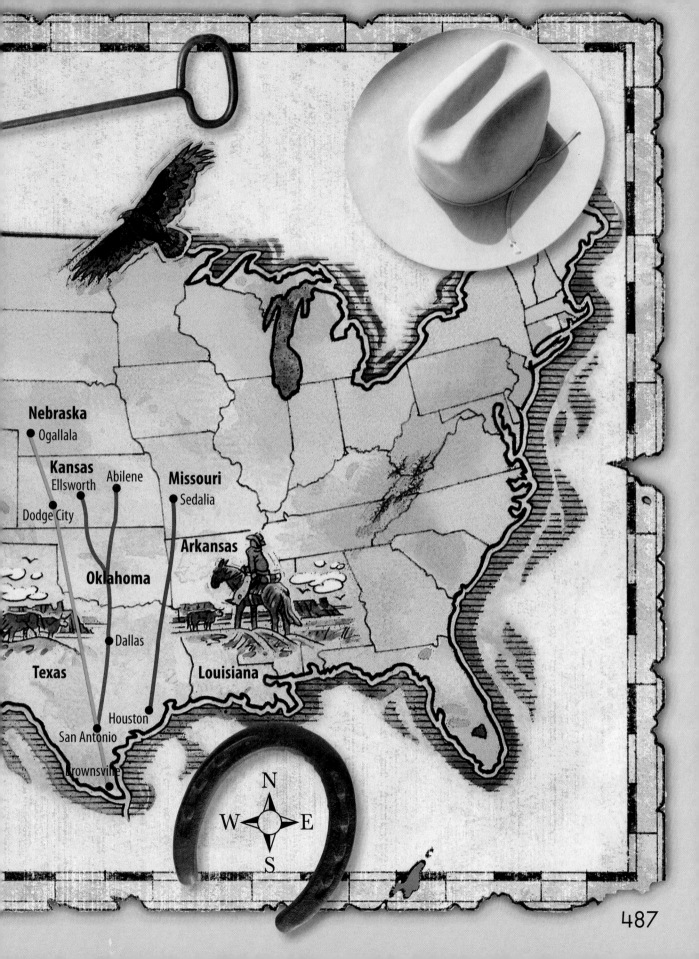

Nebraska
● Ogallala

Kansas
Ellsworth ● Abilene

Missouri
● Sedalia

Dodge City

Arkansas

Oklahoma

● Dallas

Texas

Louisiana

● Houston

San Antonio

Brownsville

N
W ◆ E
S

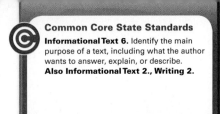
Common Core State Standards

Informational Text 6. Identify the main purpose of a text, including what the author wants to answer, explain, or describe. **Also Informational Text 2., Writing 2.**

Envision It! | Retell

Think Critically

1. In the text, cowboys took the cattle to market. How do you think today's cowboys get the cattle to market? Text to World

2. What does the author want you to know about the work cowboys did? Think Like an Author

3. What did cowboys have to do before the trail drive? Sequence

4. What events are described in the story? Are they put in time order? Text Structure

5. Look Back and Write Look back at page 474. How did hats protect cowboys? Provide evidence to support your answer.

Key Ideas and Details • Text Evidence

Meet the Author and the Illustrator

LUCILLE RECHT PENNER

Lucille Recht Penner often writes about life long ago. She likes to write about cowboys. People were adventurous and brave in the Old West. They were willing to do hard things even when they didn't know what would happen to them.

Read more books written by Lucille Recht Penner or illustrated by Ben Carter.

Wilma Mankiller: Principal Chief of the Cherokee Nation

X Marks the Spot!

BEN CARTER

Ben Carter has been an artist since he graduated from college. He is of Native American descent, and his books often draw upon his heritage.

Use the *Reader's and Writer's Notebook* to record your independent reading.

Reading Log

Common Core State Standards

Writing 8. Recall information from experiences or gather information from provided sources to answer a question. **Also Language 2.**

Expository

Key Features of a Compare-and-Contrast Text

- tells how two things are alike and how they are different
- uses clue words to show likenesses and differences

READING STREET ONLINE
GRAMMAR JAMMER
www.ReadingStreet.com

Compare-and-Contrast Text

A compare-and-contrast text tells how two things are alike and how they are different. Writers can use clue words to help them compare and contrast things. Some clue words are *both, and,* and *but.* The student model on the next page is an example of a compare-and-contrast text.

Writing Prompt Think about a job you do at home or at school. Think about tasks that cowboys did. Compare and contrast your job with a cowboy's job.

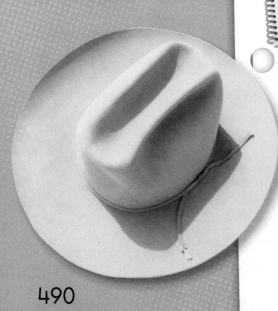

Writer's Checklist

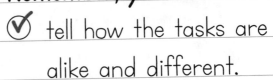
Remember, you should . . .

- ✓ tell how the tasks are alike and different.
- ✓ use clue words to help compare and contrast.
- ✓ focus on important ideas.
- ✓ use commas correctly.

Caring for Animals

Both cowboys and I care for animals. Cowboys took care of cattle, and I take care of my fish. I have to feed my fish and help clean the tank. On a trail drive, cowboys had to get cattle food, water, and rest. Cowboys made sure the cattle stayed safe.

My job takes minutes. A cowboy's job took months. Mine is easy, but a cowboy's was hard. I do my job once a day, but a cowboy worked all day.

Writer uses **commas** correctly. They separate the items *food*, *water*, and *rest*.

Writing Trait Focus Writer focuses on likenesses and differences.

Genre This **compare-and-contrast text** tells how the jobs are alike and different.

Conventions

Commas

Remember Use **commas** to separate three or more items listed together in a sentence.

- Cowboys ate **beans, biscuits,** and **steak**.

491

Common Core State Standards
Informational Text 6. Identify the main purpose of a text, including what the author wants to answer, explain, or describe.

Genre
Informational Text

- Informational text often gives facts about real people, places, and events that reflect history or the traditions of communities.

- Informational text may describe objects and their uses.

- Informational text may use pictures and headings.

- Read "Cowboy Gear." What is the topic, or the "big idea," of this text?

COWBOY GEAR

from *The Cowboy's Handbook*
★ by Tod Cody ★

A cowboy's clothes and equipment had to be hard-wearing. There was no room for luggage on the trail drive, and most cowboys wore the same thing for months. Mud-caked and smelly, these clothes were often burned at the end of the journey.

READY TO HIT THE TRAIL!

What to Wear When You're Riding the Range

HAT
You can use it to signal to other cowboys, beat trail dust off your clothes, and hold food for your horse. A true cowboy wears his hat when he's sleeping.

PANTS
Cowboys originally refused to wear jeans because they were worn by miners and farm laborers. Pants (trousers) made of thick woolen material are more comfortable to wear on horseback.

BOOTS
The pointed toes and high heels are designed for riding, not for walking. That's why cowboys in the movies walk the way they do!

BANDANNA
Soak it in water, roll it up into a wad, and place it under your hat to keep cool during a hot spell. You can also use it to filter muddy water and blindfold a "spooked" horse.

CHAPS
These thick leather leg-coverings will protect your legs from cow horns, rope burns, scrapes, and scratches. They also give a better grip to the saddle.

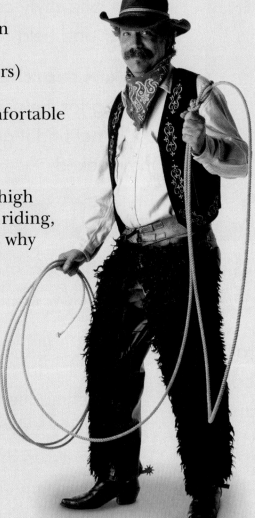

Let's **Think** About...

Why does the author tell what cowboys did with their clothing at the end of a trail drive? **Informational Text**

Let's **Think** About...

Reading Across Texts What information did each selection give about hats, bandannas, chaps, and boots?

Writing Across Texts Write a paragraph explaining which piece of gear you think cowboys needed most.

Vocabulary

Unfamiliar Words

Context Clues Look at the context clues to help find the relevant meanings of unfamiliar words.

Practice It! Use context to determine the meaning of each bold word.

1. The **bashful** child would not say hello. She shyly covered her face as her dad held her.

2. The kids **searched** the room, hunting for the next clue. But they could not find it anywhere they looked.

Fluency

Accuracy and Appropriate Rate

When reading, read all the words. Do not add or leave out words. Read at an appropriate pace. Sometimes you will want to read a little faster, for example, when something exciting is happening.

Practice It! Read the text below to a partner.

I ran in the 300-meter race at school today. I was behind the lead runner, but then I had a spurt of energy. I crossed the finish line first! This is my first-place ribbon.

Media Literacy

Notice the words that programs use to guide you through the game.

Identify Written Conventions

Some video games have number games. Some video games have word games. Some games take players from one place to another. The games use words to help players know what to do. The game starts with a title, or the name of the game. Then you may see the words *start* or *begin,* or *click here to begin.* Other words such as *pause* or *stop* may let you stop the game for a while.

Practice It! Look at a classroom computer game. Like a video game, find words that tell you what to do and how to play. Describe the game to a friend. Give the title, and tell the friend how to begin playing the game.

Tips

- For the most fun, read and follow the directions that appear on the screen when playing a computer or video game.
- Identify the written conventions that are used for the game.

495

Oral Vocabulary

Let's Talk About

Celebrated and Shared Traditions

- Share information about traditions that are shared through celebrations.

- Share ideas about traditions that are shared through special events.

READING STREET ONLINE
CONCEPT TALK VIDEO
www.ReadingStreet.com

Diploma of Graduation

Common Core State Standards

Language 4.e. Use glossaries and beginning dictionaries, both print and digital, to determine or clarify the meaning of words and phrases. **Also Language 4.**

Envision It! | Words to Know

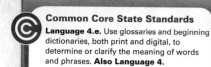

assembly

microphone

rallies

election

slogan

speeches

READING STREET ONLINE
VOCABULARY ACTIVITIES
www.ReadingStreet.com

Vocabulary Strategy for

Multiple-Meaning Words

Dictionary/Glossary When you read, you may see a word you know, but the meaning doesn't make sense in the sentence. The word may be a multiple-meaning word. You can look in a dictionary or a glossary to figure out the relevant meaning of the word.

1. Use the guide words at the top of each page to help you find the word.

2. Read the meanings given for the word.

3. Decide which meaning of the word makes sense in the sentence.

Read "Marcus and Jin." Use a dictionary or glossary to help you determine the meanings of multiple-meaning words.

Words to Write Reread "Marcus and Jin." Write at least three questions to Marcus about Washington, D.C. Use words from the *Words to Know* list.

Marcus and Jin

Marcus and Jin are friends. Marcus talked about his trip to Washington, D.C.

"It was fun," he said. "I got to see Capitol Hill. That's where members of Congress meet. It's an assembly."

Jin asked, "What do they do there?"

Marcus shrugged. "They make laws for our country," he said.

"How does someone become a member of Congress?" asked Jin.

"The country has an election. The people vote for who they want," said Marcus. "A person who wants to be in Congress has rallies. He or she gives speeches using a microphone so everyone can hear him or her talk. Then that person meets people and asks for everyone's vote. The person becomes a member if he or she gets enough votes. That person may use a slogan too."

"Why would that person use a slogan?" asked Jin.

"It helps people remember to vote for them," said Marcus.

"I wish I could visit Washington, D.C.," said Jin.

"I'm sure you will someday," said Marcus.

Your Turn!

⏸ **Need a Review?** For help with using a dictionary or glossary to find the meanings of multiple-meaning words, see *Words!* on p. W•14.

▶ **Ready to Try It?** Read *Grace for President* on pp. 504–519.

GRACE
FOR
PRESIDENT

by Kelly DiPucchio

illustrated by LeUyen Pham

504

Question of the Week

How are different traditions celebrated and shared?

One morning in September, Mrs. Barrington rolled out a big poster with all of the Presidents' pictures on it. Grace Campbell could not believe her eyes.

"Where are the **GIRLS**?"

"That is a very good question!" said Mrs. Barrington.

"The truth is, our country has never had a woman President."

"**NO** girl President? **EVER**?" Grace asked.

"No, I'm afraid not," said Mrs. Barrington.

Grace sat at her desk and stewed. No girls? Who'd ever heard of such a crazy thing?

Finally, she raised her hand.

"Yes, Grace?"

"I've been thinking it over, and I'd like to be **PRESIDENT**!"

Several students in the class laughed.

"Well, I think that's a star-spangled idea, Grace!" said Mrs. Barrington.

"In fact, we can have our own election right here at Woodrow Wilson Elementary!"

The snickering in the room stopped. Grace smiled.

"Would anyone else like to run for President?" Mrs. Barrington asked the class.

Nobody raised their hand.

Becoming President was going to be easy! Grace thought.

The next day, Mrs. Barrington made an announcement.

"In the name of **DEMOCRACY**, I have invited Mr. Waller's class to join our election.

Their class has nominated **THOMAS COBB** to be their presidential candidate!"

Grace's heart sank.

Thomas was the school spelling bee champion. His experiments always took a blue ribbon at the science fair. And he was captain of the soccer team.

Becoming President wasn't going to be so easy, after all, Grace thought.

The teachers put the names of all fifty states and the District of Columbia into a hat. Everyone except for Grace and Thomas got to choose a state.

"I'm Texas!" said Anthony.

"I'm New Hampshire!" said Rose.

"I'm Michigan," said Robbie. "What does the number 17 mean?"

"Each state is assigned a number of electoral votes. That number is determined by how many people live in that state," said Mrs. Barrington. "Each of you will be a representative for your state."

"Altogether, our country has 538 electoral votes," Mr. Waller explained. "On Election Day, the candidate who receives 270 electoral votes or more wins the election!"

"Why 270?" asked Rose.

"That's more than half of all the electoral votes," Mr. Waller said.

Becoming president REALLY wasn't going to be so easy, Grace thought.

Grace came up with a campaign slogan:

Thomas came up with his own campaign slogan:

MAKE HISTORY! VOTE
GRACE CAMPBELL
FOR PRESIDENT!

VOTE FOR
THOMAS COBB
THE BEST MAN
FOR THE JOB!

Grace listened to what issues were important to the students, and she made a list of campaign promises:

Thomas made up his own list of promises:

Grace made campaign posters and buttons.

Thomas made posters and buttons too.

Each week, the teachers set aside time for the candidates to meet with their constituents.

Polls were taken. Voters were making their choices.

Grace continued to campaign.

At recess, she gave **SPEECHES**.

During lunch, she handed out free **CUPCAKES**.

After school, she held **RALLIES**.

MEANWHILE, Thomas wasn't worried.

He had cleverly calculated that the **BOYS** held slightly more electoral votes than the **GIRLS**.

At recess, Thomas studied his spelling words.

During lunch, he worked on his latest science experiment.

After school, he played soccer.

Even before the election, Grace made good on her promises. She joined the safety squad. She organized a school beautification committee, and she volunteered her time in the school cafeteria.

In early November, Woodrow Wilson Elementary hosted a special Election Day assembly. Grace and Thomas took their places onstage as the school band began to play.

Henry was the first representative to approach the microphone.

And so it went. State after state after state cast their electoral votes. The scoreboard in the gymnasium kept track of the totals.

The voting demonstration was quickly coming to an end.

Clara approached the podium.

"The Badger State of Wisconsin casts its 10 votes for my best friend, Grace Campbell!"

Grace looked at the scoreboard.

Thomas had 268 electoral votes. She had 267.

There was only one state still unaccounted for:

WYOMING.

Thomas grinned.
Grace felt sick.

Sam walked up to the microphone.

He looked at Thomas.

He looked at Grace.

He looked down at Grace's handmade flag.

Sam didn't say a word.

"What are you waiting for?" Thomas whispered.

The band stopped playing.

All eyes were on Wyoming.

Finally, Sam cleared his throat.

"The Equality State of Wyoming casts its 3 electoral votes for . . .

GRACE CAMPBELL!!!"

517

The gymnasium erupted in
loud cheers (and a few boos).

Mrs. Barrington approached
the podium.

"With 270 electoral votes, the
winner is Grace Campbell!"

Thomas looked stunned. Grace
hugged Sam.

"Why did you do it?" she asked.

Sam handed Grace his flag.

"Because," he said, "I thought you were the best person for the job."

The following week, the students in Mrs. Barrington's class were preparing for their Career Day presentations.

Grace volunteered to go first. She stood at the front of the room and glanced at the poster still hanging on the wall.

"My name is Grace Campbell, and when I grow up, I'm going to be President of the United States."

This time, everyone believed that she would.

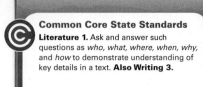

Common Core State Standards
Literature 1. Ask and answer such questions as *who, what, where, when, why,* and *how* to demonstrate understanding of key details in a text. **Also Writing 3.**

Envision It! Retell

READING STREET ONLINE
STORY SORT
www.ReadingStreet.com

Think Critically

1. In the story, Grace ran for president. Who is the President of the United States today? Text to World

2. What message does the author want you to know? Think Like an Author

3. Look back and locate three important details of America's election process. How can you find out if the details are true? Facts and Details

4. Based on the story, what prediction can you make about Grace's future? Predict and Set Purpose

5. Look Back and Write Look back at pages 508–509. Why did Grace think that becoming president was not going to be easy? Provide evidence to support your answer.

Key Ideas and Details • Text Evidence

Kelly DiPucchio

Kelly DiPucchio has many talents. When growing up, she hoped to be a professional doodler or a musical performer. As an adult, she chose to become a writer.

Ms. DiPucchio has always enjoyed children's literature. She did not start writing her own stories until after her children were born. She says that her children taught her about the importance of humor. Kelly DiPucchio is the author of more than seven children's books and continues writing stories for children today.

Read more books by Kelly DiPucchio.

Bed Hogs

What's the Magic Word?

Reading Log

Use the *Reader's and Writer's Notebook* to record your independent reading.

Key Features of a Persuasive Statement

- includes ideas to convince the reader

- uses reasons, facts, and examples

- may use persuasive words to ask for action.

READING STREET ONLINE
GRAMMAR JAMMER
www.ReadingStreet.com

...GRACE CAMPBELL!!!

Persuasive Statement

A **persuasive statement** uses reasons, facts, or examples to convince the reader to do something or to think a certain way. The student model on the next page is an example of a persuasive statement.

Writing Prompt Think about a tradition that you consider important. Write a statement to persuade people in your school or community to honor that tradition.

Writer's Checklist

Remember, you should . . .

☑ use reasons, facts, or examples to persuade.

☑ choose words to support your main idea.

☑ use commas correctly in compound sentences.

Our Map of 50 States

We like our school's new map of our state. Now I hope we can make the USA playground map look new.

The USA map is fun. We can walk to all states, but they look dull now. We run on them, and the paint is old.

Students and grown-ups in our town can help paint. This will make our school bright. It will honor our red, white, and blue nation.

The writer uses **commas** correctly in compound sentences.

Genre This **persuasive statement** supports an idea with reasons and facts.

Writing Trait Word Choice The writer uses vivid words.

Conventions

Commas in Compound Sentences

Remember Two sentences with ideas that go together can be combined by using a comma and a word such as *and* or *but*. The combined sentence is called a **compound sentence.** It has one period at the end.

Genre
Informational Text

- Informational text often gives facts about real people, places, and events that reflect history or the traditions of communities.
- Informational text usually has one topic.
- Informational text may have captions and pictures.
- Read "Home Sweet Home." Look for elements that make this an informational text.

Home Sweet Home

by Almira Astudillo Gilles

Long ago, there were no freeways or telephones, shopping malls or video games. Long ago, Native Americans were the only people in California.

Native Americans made many different kinds of homes, using materials that were easy to find. In the north, there were forests and plenty of wood for houses. The Miwok, a group that lived in Central California, had houses shaped like cones. Other houses, like those of the Chumash people of the south, were round. To build these round houses, poles made from branches were poked in the ground in a circle.

Chumash hut

Let's Think About...

What shape were the homes of the Miwok?
Informational Text

These poles were bent at the top, and smaller branches were put around them. On the outside, pieces of bushes were added. A hole in the top let air inside. When it rained, the hole was covered with animal skin.

Let's Think About...

Why does the author tell what may be inside a Native American house?
Informational Text

Inside a Native American house, you might see grass mats on the floor. You might see money made of sea snail shells. You might find moccasins and clothes of animal skins. You might find a bow and arrow for hunting. For children, there might be dolls or spinning tops made of acorns.

Families lived together in one village.

moccasins

525

Grandparents, cousins, aunts, and uncles all lived nearby. Villages could be small, with just a few families, or large, with many families. Each village had a chief who could be a man or woman.

Many Native Americans in California used acorns for food. Some groups, like the Wiyot, lived far from the oak forests. They moved their homes into the forest when it was harvest time. Men shook the oak trees to make acorns fall. Women and children picked them up.

acorns

The most important thing about a Native American home was the family inside it. Just like today, a home was a place to rest and spend time together. These houses were one big room. Families played games. Elders told stories. Adults talked about important events in the village.

Native American men sometimes built a sweathouse. The sweathouse was a place men went to heal. Inside the sweathouse there was a fire pit with stones.

Let's Think About...

What is the topic, or the "big idea," of this paragraph?
Informational Text

With the fire burning, it became very hot inside. When the men became too sweaty, they ran outside and jumped into a cool creek.

A sweathouse is made this way:

Step 1. Make a frame out of long pieces of wood.

Step 2. Put branches across the frame.

Step 3. Put thick shrubs on top of the branches.

Step 4. Cover the roof with soil. The roof should be no more than five inches thick.

sweathouse

Reading Across Texts What do you learn about community leaders in both "Home Sweet Home" and *Grace for President*? Make a chart to record your ideas.

Writing Across Texts Use your chart to write a short paragraph. Draw a conclusion about who can be leaders. Base your ideas on the selections.

Common Core State Standards
Foundational Skills 4.a. Read on-level
text with purpose and understanding.
Also Speaking/Listening 2., Language 4.e.

Let's Learn It!

Vocabulary

Multiple-Meaning Words

Dictionary/Glossary You can look the word up in a dictionary or glossary to find its relevant meaning in a sentence.

Practice It! Read each sentence. Use a dictionary or glossary to find the relevant meaning for each bold word.

1. The firefighters in the fire engine will **lead** the parade.

2. The bank keeps money in a **safe**.

3. The water in that **spring** is fresh.

Fluency

Appropriate Phrasing

When you are reading, group words together. You can use commas and end punctuation to help you group words. Try to read the words in groups. Then you will understand the reading.

Practice It! Read the text aloud.

There are many different pieces in the game of chess. Each player gets one king and one queen. Each player gets two bishops, two rooks, two knights, and eight pawns.

Listening and Speaking

Listen for a speaker's purpose and decide if the speaker meets it.

Listen for Speaker's Purpose

When giving a report, you want to communicate with your listeners. Make sure to think about your listeners as you plan your report. Let listeners know why you are giving them the information. Listeners want to know your purpose. They may ask, "Why is the speaker telling me this?" Your report should help them identify the reason for listening.

For a report, do research on your topic. Look for facts to support your ideas. You might begin a report on dog tricks with this sentence: "Dogs can do many tricks." Then the listener will know what your report is about.

As a listener, think about what the speaker is saying. Do you know what the speaker's report is about? Does the speaker support ideas with facts? Does the speaker use details to make the report interesting?

Practice It! Write a short report on a topic that interests you. Give the report to the class. Speak clearly, at an appropriate pace, and use complete sentences. While listening, identify the speaker's purpose. Explain what the purpose is when the speaker is finished.

529

Aa

adventure (ad VEN cher) An **adventure** is an exciting or unusual thing to do: Riding a raft down the river was a great **adventure**. *NOUN*

afternoon (af ter NOON) The **afternoon** is the part of the day between morning and evening: On Saturday we played all **afternoon**. *NOUN*

America (uh MAIR uh kuh) **America** is another name for North **America**. Some people use the name **America** to mean the United States. *NOUN*

annoy (uh NOI) To **annoy** is to bother or make someone feel upset or angry: Please do not **annoy** others by talking during the movie. *VERB*

assembly (uh SEM blee) An **assembly** is a group of people gathered for some purpose: The principal spoke to the school **assembly**. *NOUN*

aunt (ANT *or* AHNT) Your **aunt** is your father's sister, your mother's sister, or your uncle's wife. *NOUN*

awaken (uh WAY ken) To **awaken** is to wake up: Birds **awaken** me each morning. *VERB*

Bb

balance (BAL ens)

1. **Balance** is a steady condition or position: The gymnast lost her **balance** and fell. *NOUN*

2. To **balance** something is to put or keep something in a steady or stable condition: She **balanced** a basketball on her finger. *VERB*

bank[1] (BANGK) A **bank** is a place where people keep their money: My brother has a **bank** for nickels and pennies. *NOUN*

bank[2] (BANGK) The **bank** of a river or lake is the ground beside it: He fished from the **bank**. *NOUN*

bases (BAY sez)

1. A **base** is the bottom of something: The metal **bases** of the floor lamps might scratch the floor. *NOUN*

2. A **base** is also an object in some games: After hitting a home run, the player ran the **bases**. *NOUN*

basket (BASS kit)

1. A **basket** is something to carry or store things in: **Baskets** are made of straw, plastic, or other materials. *NOUN*

2. In basketball a **basket** is used as a goal: The **basket** is made of a metal ring with a net hanging from it. *NOUN*

basket

birthday (BERTH day) A **birthday** is the day that a person was born or something was started: Our country's **birthday** is July 4th. *NOUN*

blame (BLAYM) To **blame** is to hold someone responsible for something bad or wrong. *VERB*

building (BIL ding) A **building** is something that has been built: A **building** has walls and a roof. Schools, houses, and barns are **buildings**. *NOUN*

building

531

bumpy • clearing

bumpy (BUHM pee) If something is **bumpy**, it is rough or has a lot of bumps: This sidewalk is too **bumpy** to skate on. *ADJECTIVE*

burning (BERN ing) **Burning** means to be on fire: The campers enjoyed watching the **burning** logs. *ADJECTIVE*

Cc

campfire (KAMP fyr) A **campfire** is an outdoor fire used for cooking or staying warm. *NOUN*

canyons (KAN yuhnz) A **canyon** is a narrow valley with high steep sides, sometimes with a stream at the bottom: There are many **canyons** to visit in the western states of America. *NOUN*

cattle (KAT uhl) **Cattle** are animals raised for their meat, milk, or skins: Cows and bulls are **cattle**. *NOUN PLURAL*

chased (CHAYST) When you **chase** someone or something, you run after it: The children **chased** the ball down the hill. *VERB*

cheers (CHEERZ) When you **cheer**, you call out or yell loudly to show you like something: She **cheers** for her team. *VERB*

chewing

chewing (CHOO ing) When you **chew** something, you crush it with your teeth: He was **chewing** the nuts. *VERB*

clearing (KLEER ing) A **clearing** is an open space of land in a forest: We came to a **clearing** on our nature walk through the forest. *NOUN*

cliffs (KLIFZ) A **cliff** is a very steep, rocky slope: Climbers must be very careful on **cliffs**. *NOUN*

climbed (KLYMD) When you **climb**, you go up something, usually by using your hands and feet: The children **climbed** into the bus. *VERB*

clubhouse (KLUB HOWSS) A **clubhouse** is a building used by a group of people joined together for some special reason. *NOUN*

collects (kuh LEKTS) If you **collect** things, you bring them together or gather them together: The student **collects** the crayons. *VERB*

complain (kuhm PLAYN) To **complain** is to say that you are unhappy about something: Some people **complain** about the weather. *VERB*

coral (KOR uhl) The hard substance formed from the skeletons of tiny sea animals is **coral**: Many islands in the Pacific Ocean started as large piles of living and dead **coral**. *NOUN*

cowboy (KOW boi) A **cowboy** is a person who works on a cattle ranch: **Cowboys** also take part in rodeos. *NOUN*

crashed (KRASHD) To **crash** is to fall, hit, and be damaged with force and a loud noise: The car **crashed** into a stop sign. *VERB*

cowboy

533

dripping • freedom

Dd

dripping (DRIP ing) When something **drips**, it falls in drops: The rain was **dripping** on the roof. *VERB*

Ee

election (i LEK shuhn) An election is an act of choosing by vote: In our city we have an election for mayor every two years. *NOUN*

exploring (ek SPLOR ing) When you are **exploring**, you are traveling to discover new areas: Astronauts are **exploring** outer space. *VERB*

Ff

favorite (FAY vuhr it)

1. Your **favorite** thing is the one you like better than all the others: What is your **favorite** color? *ADJECTIVE*

2. A **favorite** is a person or thing that you like very much: Pizza is a **favorite** with me. *NOUN*

field (FEELD) A **field** is a piece of land used for a special purpose: The football **field** needs to be mowed. *NOUN*

flag (FLAG) A **flag** is a piece of colored cloth with stars or other symbols on it: Every country and state has its own **flag**. *NOUN*

flag

freedom (FREE duhm) **Freedom** is not being under someone else's control or rule. *NOUN*

fruit

fruit (FROOT) **Fruit** is the part of a tree, bush, or vine that has seeds in it and is good to eat: Apples, oranges, and strawberries are **fruit**. *NOUN*

Gg

galloped (GAL uhpt) To **gallop** is to run very fast: The horse **galloped** down the road. *VERB*

grabbed (GRABD) When you **grab** something, you take it suddenly: The dog **grabbed** the bone. *VERB*

grains (GRAYNZ) **Grains** are tiny pieces or particles: There are millions of **grains** of sand on the beach. *NOUN*

greatest (GRAYT est) If something is the **greatest**, it is the best and most important: He thought it was the **greatest** book he had ever read. *ADJECTIVE*

Hh

harvest (HAR vist)

1. A **harvest** is the ripe crops that are picked after the growing season is over: The corn **harvest** was poor after the hot, dry summer. *NOUN*

2. When you **harvest**, you gather in the crops and store them: We **harvest** the apples in late fall. *VERB*

herd • mumbles

herd (HERD) A **herd** is a group of the same kind of animals: We saw a **herd** of cows when we drove through the country. *NOUN*

herd

Ii

idea (eye DEE uh) An **idea** is a thought or plan: The class had different **ideas** on how to spend the money. *NOUN*

important (im PORT uhnt) Something that is **important** has a lot of meaning or worth: Learning to read is **important**. *ADJECTIVE*

Mm

masks (MASKS) **Masks** are coverings that hide or protect your face: The firefighters wear **masks** to help them breathe. *NOUN*

materials (muh TIR ee uhlz) **Materials** are what a thing is made from or used for: Wood and steel are building **materials.** *NOUN*

microphone (MY kruh fon) A **microphone** is an electrical device that makes your voice sound louder: People who work in television and radio stations use a **microphone**. *NOUN*

mountain (MOWN tuhn) A **mountain** is a very high hill. Some people enjoy climbing **mountains** in their free time. *NOUN*

mumbles (MUHM buhls) Someone who **mumbles** speaks too quietly to be heard clearly: When John **mumbles,** I can't understand what he is saying. *VERB*

Nn

nicknames (NIK naymz) **Nicknames** are names used instead of real names: Ed is a **nickname** for Edward. *NOUN*

Pp

particles (PAR tuh kuhls) **Particles** are very tiny pieces: The table had **particles** of dust on top. *NOUN*

perfect (PER fikt) When something is **perfect**, it is without any faults or mistakes. Larry had a **perfect** spelling test. *ADJECTIVE*

plate (PLAYT)
1. A **plate** is a dish that is almost flat and is usually round: We eat food from **plates**. *NOUN*
2. A **plate** is a hard rubber slab that a baseball player stands beside to hit the ball. *NOUN*

P.M. (PEE EM) These letters stand for *post meridiem,* which means "after midday." **P.M.** refers to the time between noon and 11:59 at night.

pond (POND) A **pond** is a body of still water that is smaller than a lake: My neighbor has a duck **pond** in his backyard. *NOUN*

practice (PRAK tiss) A **practice** is a training session: Coach says that to play the game, you must go to **practice**. *NOUN*

present

present¹ (PREZ uhnt) Another word for **present** is *here*. If you are **present**, you are not absent: Every member of the class is **present** today. *ADJECTIVE*

present² (PREZ uhnt) A **present** is a gift. A **present** is something that someone gives you or that you give someone: His uncle sent him a birthday **present**. *NOUN*

prize (PREYEZ) A **prize** is something you win for doing something well: **Prizes** will be given for the best stories. *NOUN*

Qq

quickly (KWIK lee) **Quickly** means in a short time: When I asked him a question, he answered **quickly**. *ADVERB*

Rr

railroad (RAYL rohd) A **railroad** is a system of trains, tracks, stations, and other property run by a transportation company: The cattle pens were near the **railroad** tracks. *NOUN*

rainbow

rainbow (RAYN bo) A **rainbow** is a curved band of many colors in the sky. A **rainbow** often appears when the sun shines right after it rains. *NOUN*

rallies (RAL eez) **Rallies** are meetings of many people for a specific purpose: We all attended the **rallies** in support of the candidate for President. *NOUN*

rattle (RAT uhl) To **rattle** is to make short, sharp sounds: The wind made the door **rattle**. *VERB*

538

roar (ROR) A **roar** is a loud, deep sound: The **roar** of the lion frightened some people at the zoo. *NOUN*

root (ROOT) The **root** is the part of a plant that grows underground: A plant gets food and water through its **roots**. *NOUN*

Ss

sailed (SAYLD) When something **sails**, it travels on the water or through the air: The ball **sailed** out of the ballpark. *VERB*

seeps (SEEPS) When something **seeps,** it soaks through or passes through an opening very slowly in small amounts: Water **seeps** into our basement after heavy rains. *VERB*

shrugs (SHRUHGZ) To **shrug** is to raise your shoulders briefly to show that you are not interested or do not know: Every time I ask my brother if he wants to play, he just **shrugs.** *VERB*

signature (SIG nuh chur) Your **signature** is the way you sign your name: Each student needed a parent's **signature** on the permission slip. *NOUN*

signmaker (SYN mayk er) A **signmaker** makes marks or words on a sign that give information or tell you what to do or not to do. *NOUN*

slivers (SLIV uhrz) A **sliver** is a long, thin piece that has been split off or broken off. He ate a **sliver** of cheese before dinner. *NOUN*

Glossary

slogan • spilling

slogan (SLO guhn) A **slogan** is a word or phrase used by a business, political party, or any group to make its purpose known: "Lunch served in 30 minutes or it's free" was the restaurant's **slogan**. *NOUN*

smooth (SMOOTH) When something is **smooth**, it has an even surface. Something that is **smooth** is not bumpy or rough: The road was very **smooth**. *ADJECTIVE*

soil¹ (SOIL) **Soil** is the top layer of the Earth. **Soil** is dirt: Our garden has such rich **soil** that almost anything will grow in it. *NOUN*

soil² (SOIL) If you **soil** something, you make it dirty: The dust will **soil** her white gloves. *VERB*

speeches (SPEECH es)

1. **Speech** is the act of talking: People express their thoughts by **speech**. *NOUN*

2. A **speech** is a formal talk to a group of people: The President gave an excellent **speech**. *NOUN*

spilling (SPIL ing) To **spill** is to let something fall out or run out of its container: Dad knocked the saltshaker over, **spilling** salt on the table. *VERB*

soil

splashing (SPLASH ing) To **splash** is to cause liquid to fly about and get others wet: The swimmers are **splashing** each other with water. *VERB*

splashing

stars (STARZ)

1. **Stars** are the very bright points of light that shine in the sky at night: On a clear night, the **stars** are very bright. *NOUN*

2. **Stars** are shapes that have five or six points: I drew **stars** on the paper. *NOUN*

station (STAY shuhn) A **station** is a building or place used for a special reason: The man went to the police **station**. *NOUN*

stripes (STRYPS) **Stripes** are long, narrow bands of color: Our flag has seven red **stripes** and six white **stripes**. *NOUN*

substances (SUHB stan sez) A **substance** is something that has weight and takes up space: Solids, liquids, and powders are examples of **substances.** *NOUN*

suffer (SUHF ur)To **suffer** is to have or feel pain, grief, or injury: She **suffered** a broken leg while skiing. *VERB*

sway (SWAY) To **sway** is to swing or cause to swing back and forth, side to side, or to one side: The dancers **sway** to the music. *VERB*

Tt

threw

texture (TEKS chur) **Texture** is the look and feel of something, especially its roughness or smoothness. *NOUN*

threw (THROO) When you **threw** something, you sent it through the air:
She **threw** the ball back to him. *VERB*

tightly (TYT lee) When something is tied **tightly**, it is firmly tied: The rope was tied **tightly** around the ladders on the truck. *ADVERB*

townspeople (TOWNZ pee puhl) **Townspeople** are the men, women, and children who live in a village or town: The **townspeople** enjoyed the fair. *NOUN*

trails (TRAYLZ) **Trails** are paths across fields or through the woods: Two **trails** led to the river. *NOUN*

traveled (TRAV uhld) To **travel** is to go from one place to another: He **traveled** in Europe this past summer. *VERB*

treat (TREET) A **treat** is a gift of food, drink, a free ticket, or the like: She gave us **treats** on the last day of school. *NOUN*

truest (TROO ist) To be **true** is to be faithful and loyal: She is the **truest** friend I have. *ADJECTIVE*

Vv

vine (VYN) A **vine** is a plant that grows along the ground. Some **vines** climb up walls and fences: Pumpkins, melons, and grapes grow on **vines**. *NOUN*

vine

volcano (vol KAY no) A **volcano** is a cone-shaped hill or mountain that has an opening through which lava, rock fragments, and gas are forced out from the Earth's crust: They feared the **volcano** would erupt. *NOUN*

Ww

wagged (WAGD) To **wag** is to move from side to side or up and down: The dog **wagged** her tail. *VERB*

whisper (WIS puhr) To **whisper** is to speak very softly and gently: Children **whisper** secrets to each other. *VERB*

wondered (WUHN derd) When you **wondered** about something, you wanted to know about it: He **wondered** what time it was. *VERB*

Unit 4

A Froggy Fable

English	Spanish
clearing	*claro
crashed	chocó
perfect	*perfecto
pond	estanque
spilling	soltando
splashing	salpicando
traveled	viajaron

Life Cycle of a Pumpkin

English	Spanish
bumpy	desiguales
fruit	fruta
harvest	cosecha
root	raíz
smooth	lisas
soil	tierra
vine	enredadera

Soil

English	Spanish
grains	granos
materials	*materiales
particles	*partículas
seeps	se filtra
substances	*sustancias
texture	*textura

The Night the Moon Fell

English	Spanish
balance	equilibrio
canyons	cañones
coral	*coral
rattle	repiquetear
slivers	astillas
sway	mecer
whisper	susurrar

* English/Spanish Cognate: A **cognate** is a word that is similar in two languages and has the same meaning in both languages.

The First Tortilla

English	Spanish
awaken	despertar
cliffs	acantilados
mountain	montaña
prize	premio
rainbow	arcoiris
suffer	*sufrir
volcano	*volcán

Unit 5

Fire Fighter!

English	Spanish
building	edificio
burning	ardiente
masks	máscaras
quickly	rápidamente
roar	rugido
station	*estación
tightly	firmemente

Carl the Complainer

English	Spanish
annoy	enojar
complain	quejarse
mumbles	dice entre dientes
P.M.	*P.M.
shrugs	se encoje de hombros
signature	firma

Bad Dog, Dodger!

English	Spanish
chased	persiguieron
chewing	mordiendo
dripping	goteando
grabbed	agarró
practice	entrenamiento
treat	galletas (de perro)
wagged	meneó

Horace and Morris but mostly Dolores

English	Spanish
adventure	*aventura
climbed	subieron
clubhouse	casa del club
exploring	*explorando
greatest	mejores
truest	más verdaderos
wondered	se preguntaba

The Signmaker's Assistant

English	Spanish
afternoon	tarde
blame	culpen
idea	*idea
important	*importante
signmaker	rotulista
townspeople	ciudadanos

Unit 6
Just Like Josh Gibson

English	Spanish
bases	*bases
cheers	gritos de entusiasmo
field	campo
plate	base
sailed	volaban
threw	tiró

Red, White, and Blue: The Story of the American Flag

English	Spanish
America	Estados Unidos
birthday	cumpleaños
flag	bandera
freedom	libertad
nicknames	apodos
stars	estrellas
stripes	franjas

A Birthday Basket for Tía

English	Spanish
aunt	tía
bank	alcancía
basket	cesta
collects	recoge
favorite	* favorito
present	regalo

Cowboys

English	Spanish
campfire	fuego (de campamento)
cattle	ganado
cowboy	vaquero
galloped	galoparon
herd	manada
railroad	ferrocarril
trails	sendas

Grace for President

English	Spanish
assembly	reunión
election	* elección
microphone	* micrófono
rallies	mitin
slogan	* eslogan
speeches	discursos

Text

Grateful acknowledgment is made to the following for copyrighted material:

Atheneum Books for Young Readers an imprint of Simon & Schuster Children's Publishing Division

"Horace and Morris But Mostly Delores" from *Horace And Morris But Mostly Delores* by James Howe, illustrated by Amy Walrod. Text copyright © 1999 by James Howe, illustrations copyright © 1999 by Amy Walrod. Reprinted with permission of Atheneum Books for Young Readers, an imprint of Simon and Schuster Children's Publishing Division. All rights reserved.

Breslich & Foss/Cobblehill Books an affiliate of Dutton Children's Books a div of Penguin Group (USA)

From *The Cowboy's Handbook* by Tod Cody, copyright © 1996 by Breslich & Foss. Used by permission of Cobblehill Books, an affiliate of Dutton Children's Books, A Division of Penguin Young Readers Group, A Member of Penguin Group (USA) Inc., 345 Hudson Street, New York, NY 10014. All rights reserved.

Candlewick Press

"A Froggy Fable" by John Lechner. Copyright © 2005 by John Lechner. Reproduced by permission of the publisher, Candlewick Press, Somerville, MA.

Dial Books for Young Readers a div of Penguin Group (USA)

"How Do Seeds Know Which Way Is Up?" from *Where Do Fish Go In Winter and Other Great Mysteries* by Amy Goldman Koss, copyright © 1987 by Amy Goldman Koss. "The Signmaker's Assistant" by Tedd Arnold. Copyright © 1992 by Tedd Arnold. Used by permission of Dial Books for Young Readers, A Division of Penguin Young Readers Group, A Member of Penguin Group (USA) Inc., 345 Hudson Street, New York, NY 10014. All rights reserved.

Disney Book Group a div of Hyperion Books for Children

From *Grace For President* by Kelly DiPucchio. Text copyright © 2008 by Kelly DiPucchio. Illustrations copyright © 2008 by LeUyen Pham. Reprinted by permission of Disney Book Group. All rights reserved.

Dorling Kindersley Limited

"Fire Fighter!" by Angela Royston. Copyright © 1998 Dorling Kindersley Limited, London. Reprinted by permission.

Grosset & Dunlap a div of Penguin Group (USA)

"Cowboys" by Lucille Recht Penner. Text copyright © Lucille Recht Penner, 1996. Illustrations copyright © Ben Carter, 1996. "Red, White, and Blue" by John Herman. Text copyright © 1998 by John Herman. Illustrations copyright © 1998 by Robin Roraheck. All Aboard Reading and Grosset and Dunlap are trademarks of Penguin Group (USA) Inc. All rights reserved. Published by arrangement with Grosset & Dunlap, a division of Penguin Young Readers Group, a member of Penguin Group (USA) Inc. All rights reserved.

Heinemann Publishers Ltd. (UK) & Harcourt Education Limited

"Life Cycle of a Pumpkin" from *Life Cycle Of A Pumpkin* by Ron Fridell. Used by permission.

House of Anansi Press, Ltd. & Groundwood Books

"The Night The Moon Fell" by Pat Mora. Text copyright © 2000 by Pat Mora. Illustrations copyright © 2000 by Domi. First published in Canada and the United States © 2000 by Groundwood Books Ltd. La Noche Que Se Cayo Le Luna by Pat Mora. © 2000 Texto dePat Mora. © 2000 Illustraciones de Domi. © 2000 Traduccion de Claudia M. Lee. Un Libro Tigrillo. Translation of "The Night the Moon Fell." First published in Canada and the United States © 2000 by Groundwood Books. Used by permission.

KidParties.com/Daric Systems, Inc

"Family Traditions: Birthdays" (Originally titled Birthday Traditions from Around the World) from WWW.KIDPARTIES.COM/TRADITIONS.HTM. Copyright ©1997-2009 Daric Systems, Inc., All rights reserved. Reprinted by permission.

Lerner Publishing Group, Inc

"Carl the Complainer" by Michelle Knudson and illustrated by Maryann Cocca-Leffler. Text copyright © 2005 by Kane Press, Inc.

Illustrations copyright © 2005 by Maryann Cocca-Leffler. "Soil" from *Soil* by Sally M. Walker. Copyright © 2007 by Sally Walker. Used by permission of Lerner Publishing Group, Inc. All rights reserved. No part of this text excerpt may be used or reproduced in any manner whatsoever without the prior written permission of Lerner Publishing Group, Inc.

Margaret K. McElderry Books an imprint of Simon & Schuster Children's Publishing Division

Reprinted with the permission of Margaret K. McElderry Books, an imprint of Simon & Schuster Children's Publishing Division from *Bad Dog, Dodger!* by Barbara Abercrombie. Text Copyright © 2002 Barbara Abercrombie.

*Santillana USA Publishing Company, Inc

"Fishermen" by Juan Bautista Grosso from *Singing Horse* by Alma Flor Ada and F. Isabel Campoy. Text copyright © 2000 Alma Flor Ada and F. Isabel Campoy. Illustrations by Claudia Legnazzi. Edition Copyright © 2000 Santillana USA Publishing Company, Inc.

Simon & Schuster Books for Young Readers an imprint of Simon & Schuster Children's Publishing Division

"A Birthday Basket for Tia" from *A Birthday Basket For Tia* by Pat Mora, illustrated by Cecily Lang. Text copyright © 1992 by Pat Mora, Illustrations copyright © 1992 by Cecily Lang. From *Just Like Josh Gibson* by Angela Johnson, illustrated by Beth Peck. Text copyright © 2004 by Angela Johnson, illustrations copyright © 2004 Beth Peck. Reprinted with permission of Simon & Schuster Books for Young Readers, an Imprint of Simon & Schuster Children's Publishing Division. All rights reserved.

Simon Spotlight an imprint of Simon & Schuster Children's Publishing Division

Reprinted with the permission of Simon Spotlight, an imprint of Simon & Schuster Children's Publishing Division from *Wind* by Marion Dane Bauer. Copyright © 2003 Marion Dane Bauer.

Susan Bergholz Literary Services

"The First Tortilla" by Rudolfo Anaya. Text copyright © 2007 by Rudolfo Anaya. Illustrations copyright © 2007 by Amy Cordova. Published by the University of New Mexico Press. Used by permission of Susan Bergholz Literary Services, New York, NY and Lamy, NM. All rights reserved.

Note: Every effort has been made to locate the copyright owner of material reproduced on this component. Omissions brought to our attention will be corrected in subsequent editions.

*Domestic Edition Only

Cover: (C)©Jupiterimages/Getty Images, (TR) ©Kim Karpeles/Alamy Images, (TC) ©lassendesignen/Fotolia, (TL) TongRo Image Stock, (BC) ©Benshot/Fotolia

Illustrations

EI2–EI15 Robert Neubecker; **28–41** Wednesday Kirwan; **46–51** Ariel Pang; **216–276** Laura Ovresat; **235** Maryann Cocca-Leffler; **266–278** Diane Greenseid; **386–389** Clint Hansen; **400–416** Shannan Stirnweiss; **412** Derek Grinnell; **W2–W15** Alessia Girasole

Photographs

Every effort has been made to secure permission and provide appropriate credit for photographic material. The publisher deeply regrets any omission and pledges to correct errors called to its attention in subsequent editions.

Unless otherwise acknowledged, all photographs are the property of Pearson Education, Inc.

Photo locators denoted as follows: Top (T), Center (C), Bottom (B), Left (L), Right (R), Background (Bkgd)

CVR (Blue sky) TongRo Image Stock/Fotosearch; **CVR** (Plants) Benshot/Fotolia; **CVR** (Garden) Jupiter Images/Getty Images; **4** Larry Mulvehill/Corbis; **8** Jim Sugar/Corbis; **12** Mira/Alamy; **16** (C) ellenamani/Fotolia; **18** Larry Mulvehill/Corbis; **19** (C) Andrea Jones Images/Alamy; **19** (TR) Tony Freeman/Photo Edit; **20–21** (Bkgd) Don. B. Stevenson/Alamy; **20** (B) Steven Georges/Press-Telegram/Corbis; **21** PM Images/Getty Images; **25** Jupiter Images/Getty Images; **26, 541** keller/Fotolia; **26** (C) Jordan

WORDS! | Vocabulary Handbook

Antonyms

Synonyms

Base Words

Prefixes

Suffixes

Context Clues

Related Words

Compound Words

Multiple-Meaning Words

Homographs

Homonyms

Homophones

Dictionary/Glossary

Thesaurus

Antonyms

Antonyms are words that have opposite meaning. *Messy* and *neat* are antonyms.

Messy

Neat

Antonyms can be used to contrast two things. Antonyms help readers understand differences.

Synonyms

Synonyms are words that have the same meaning or similar meaning. *Happy* and *glad* are synonyms.

Happy

Glad

Knowing and using synonyms can help make your writing more interesting. Look in a thesaurus to find synonyms.

Base Words

A base word is a word that cannot be broken down into smaller words or word parts. *Appear* and *cloud* are base words.

Appear

Knowing the meaning of a base word can help you understand the meaning of longer words.

Cloud

Prefixes

A prefix is a word part that can be added to the beginning of a base word. In the word *disappear, dis-* is a prefix.

Appear

Disappear

Knowing the meaning of a prefix can help you figure out the meaning of the new word.

Common Prefixes and Their Meanings

un-	not
re-	again, back
in-	not
dis-	not, opposite of
pre-	before

Suffixes

A suffix is a word part added to the end of a base word. In the word *cloudless, -less* is a suffix.

Cloud

Cloudless

Common Suffixes and Their Meanings

-able	can be done
-ment	action or process
-less	without
-tion	act, process

Knowing how a suffix changes a word can help you figure out the meaning of the new word.

Context Clues

Read the words before and after a word that you don't know to help you make sense of it.

I saw a robin, a bluebird, a sapsucker, and a turkey while walking in the woods.

Related Words

Related words are words that have the same base word. *Bicycle*, *recycle*, and *cyclone* are related words. They all have the base word *cycle*.

Bicycle

Cyclone

Recycle

If you know what the base word means, you may be able to figure out the meaning of words related to it.

Compound Words

Compound words are words made of two smaller words. *Goldfish* and *basketball* are compound words.

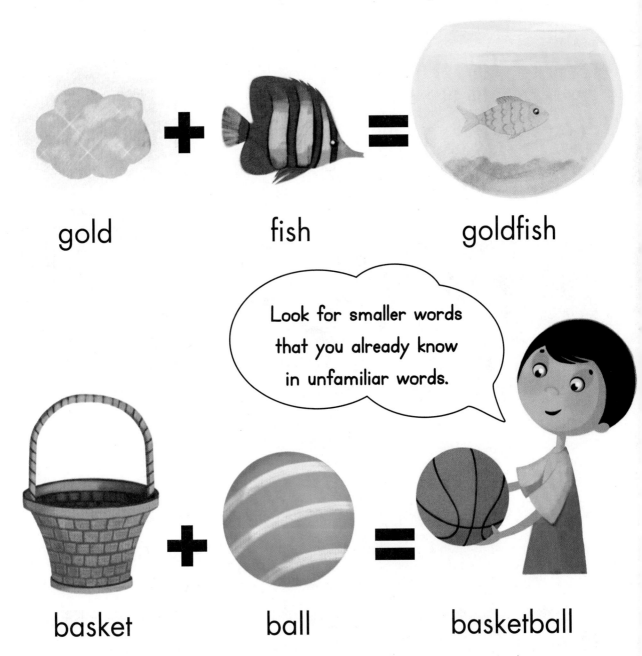

gold   fish   goldfish

Look for smaller words that you already know in unfamiliar words.

basket   ball   basketball

Multiple-Meaning Words

Multiple-meaning words are words that can have different meanings depending on how they are used.

Homographs

Homographs are words that are spelled the same. They have different meanings, and they may be pronounced the same way or differently.

Bow

Bow

Read the words before and after a homograph to discover its meaning and pronunciation. Check a dictionary to be sure.

Homonyms

Homonyms are words that are spelled the same. They have different meanings, and they are pronounced the same way.

Pen

You can figure out the meaning of a homonym by reading the words around it.

Pen

Homophones

Homophones are words that sound the same, but they are spelled differently and they have different meanings.

Night

Knight

Homophones might be confusing when you hear them being read aloud. Pay attention to the words before and after the homophone to find its meaning.

Understanding
Homographs, Homonyms, and Homophones

	Pronunciation	Spelling	Meaning
Homographs	may be the same or different	same	different
Homonyms	same	same	different
Homophones	same	different	different

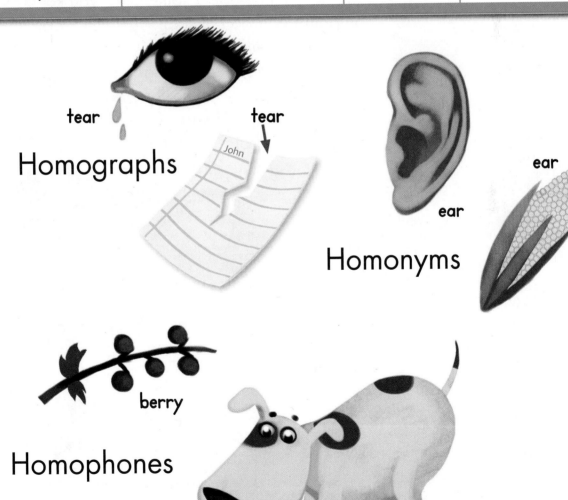

tear

tear

Homographs

ear

ear

Homonyms

berry

Homophones

bury

Dictionary/Glossary

A dictionary and a glossary are books that explain the words of our language. Both books put the words in alphabetical order. A glossary can be found at the back of a book.

continue: ① (kuhn TIN yoo)
② 1. If you continue doing something, you keep on going and do not stop: ③ *These roads continue for miles.* ④ [verb]
2. To continue also means to go on with something after stopping for a while: *The teacher said that she would continue the story tomorrow.* [verb]
⑤ **-continues, continued, continuing.**

① This part of the entry shows you how to pronounce the word.

② Here is the word's definition.

③ The word is used in an example to help you understand its meaning.

④ The dictionary or glossary entry tells you the word's part of speech. *Continue* is a verb.

⑤ See how the word changes when it has a suffix added.

Thesaurus

A thesaurus is a book of synonyms. The words in a thesaurus are in alphabetical order.

sleep verb

be asleep, nap, doze, snooze, catch a few z's, take a siesta, catnap

Keep a thesaurus handy when you write. It can help you find just the right word.